Wilderness Canoeing

A Guide to the Boundary Waters of Minnesota

Rich Annen

M&B Global Solutions, Inc.
Green Bay, Wisconsin (USA)

Wilderness Canoeing
A Guide to the Boundary Waters of Minnesota

© 2017 Richard Annen

First Edition
All Rights Reserved. The author grants no assignable permission to reproduce for resale or redistribution. This license is limited to the individual purchaser and does not extend to others. Permission to reproduce these materials for any other purpose must be obtained in writing from the publisher except for the use of brief quotations within book chapters.

Disclaimer
The views expressed in this work are solely those of the author and do not necessarily reflect the views of the publisher, and the publisher hereby disclaims any responsibility for them. In the event you use any of the information in this book for yourself, which is your constitutional right, the author and the publisher assume no responsibility for your actions. All information contained in this book with regard to websites, phone numbers and operating businesses was accurate as of this writing and cannot be guaranteed in perpetuity.

Cover photos by the author

For additional information and photos, please visit:
http://borealfyr.com/

ISBN 10: 1-942731-25-6
ISBN 13: 978-1-942731-25-2

Printed by Seaway Printing, Green Bay, Wisconsin

Published by M&B Global Solutions Inc.
Green Bay, Wisconsin (USA)

Dedication

I would like to dedicate this book to the preservers of the wilderness. From John Muir and the Sierra Club for initiating awareness to the need to preserve our natural resources way back when no one could see its beauty. To President Theodore Roosevelt for his foresight to federally protect public lands. To Sigurd Olsen for his efforts in establishing the Boundary Waters area as a wilderness. To Dave and Amy Freeman for their recent efforts in bringing attention to the outside threats to the Boundary Waters. To Save the Boundary Waters for their work in organizing a campaign to protect the Boundary Waters from mining interests.

But most importantly, I dedicate this book to you and all the users of the wilderness for your efforts in its preservation every time you are there.

Enjoy, don't destroy

Contents

Introduction 1
Preface 3
  1. Getting Acquainted with the Area 5
  2. Before You Go 23
  3. Planning Your Trip 53
  4. Equipment 69
  5. Meals 97
  6. Traveling in the Wilderness 113
  7. Establishing Your Camp 129
  8. Activities 141
  9. Trips 157
10. While You're in the Area 171
Appendix 1 - First Aid Kit 181
Appendix 2 - Entry Points 183
Appendix 3 - Quetico Provincial Park 186
Appendix 4 - Outfitters 188
Appendix 5 - Clothing 196
Appendix 6 - Camp Gear 200
Appendix 7 - Cook Gear 201
Appendix 8 - Personal Gear 202
Appendix 9 - Meal Suggestions 204
Appendix 10 - Fishing Tackle 213
Appendix 11 - Contacts / Resources 215
Acknowledgements 218
About the Author 219

Introduction

I was born in Madison, Wisconsin, the last of eleven children. My older siblings began a tradition of camping that continues after more than fifty years. We still hold an annual campout for our family reunion.

Every summer my wife, Mary, and I would load up our three sons and head out in a different direction. Over the years we have been coast to coast in both the United States and Canada. We have been to most of the major national parks and many of the mountain ranges.

When not traveling afar, we would spend our summers on trips in the upper Midwest. Backpacking trips to Upper Michigan's Porcupine Mountains and Isle Royale National Park. River trips on the Wolf, Kickapoo, Flambeau, St. Croix, and Wisconsin. Canoe trips in the Sylvania Wilderness in Ottawa National Forest and, of course, to the Boundary Waters Canoe Area Wilderness in Superior National Forest. I took my first trip to the Boundary Waters in 1983 with my wife. Since then I have been back many times. The place has a magnetism I find hard to resist.

The reason I mentioned the above trips is to show you I have some practical experience. I think I have been in most situations one can imagine while camping. From a tropical storm while at First Landing State Park on the Chesapeake Bay, to fourteen inches of snow while deer hunting from a tent in northern Wisconsin. From 104-degree summer heat to 20-below wind chills in the winter.

Throughout this book I will relate to you some of the different ways of equipping, traveling, cooking, or setting up your camp. Not all will agree with what the "experts" say. Some may even be contrary to the United States Forest Service recommendations. All have been used and proven over time. I don't disagree with the experts or the Forest Service, I just believe there are options and sometimes you can do things differently.

The photos in this book were taken by me or members of the "corps," my family and friends who have accompanied me during our numerous trips to the Boundary Waters and on many a wilderness adventure. (For additional information and photos, please visit my website at http://borealfyr.com.)

"There is in my nature, methinks, a singular yearning toward all wilderness."

- Henry David Thoreau

Preface

The focus of this book is to give a novice wilderness canoeist some guidance in traveling and camping in the wilderness. It is intended for the beginner who wants to enjoy the Boundary Waters area but who isn't keen on buying all the expensive equipment. It is not intended for the experienced outdoorsman planning an expedition. In this book I will relate to you how we outfit our group and give you some basic direction on having a safe and enjoyable trip.

I write this book with reluctance. There have been many good books written about the Boundary Waters area. In my readings I find that many of the writers are avid, knowledgeable, and competent backcountry enthusiasts who can spend weeks or months in the wilderness. There are books on canoeing, wilderness camping, equipment selection, preplanned trips, meals, and survival. In addition, you can get books on its geology, wildlife, history, natives, and settlers. And if that isn't enough, the internet has message boards and blogs. There is more information than one can digest.

If this is to be your first wilderness expedition, and perhaps your only one, I suggest using the services of an outfitter. If you have some camping equipment, you may opt for partial outfitting and let the outfitter provide you with the items you don't have. If you are traveling to the area from some distance, it may be easier to let the outfitter provide the bulkier items. Many regular campers to the area use outfitters for this reason.

The role of the outfitter goes way beyond equipment. They are knowledgeable and experienced in camping in the Boundary Waters area. They can help you plan a trip that meets your experience and desires. If you enjoyed your experience and wish to repeat it, you can then weigh the cost of buying your own equipment. During your trip(s), ask around and notice how others travel and camp. This will give you an idea of what equipment you may want to purchase.

The wilderness is, well, a wilderness. It should not be taken lightly. I hope that this book will give you an awareness of some of the difficulties you may endure, and the knowledge and preparedness to meet them. Most, if not all (hopefully) of your trip will offer you no challenges. But there is a potential for situations to arise that will require you to find a solution that will keep you safe. If you screw up, chances are you will be uncomfortable for a while.

I have read numerous articles about people lost in the wilderness. I'm not talking about disasters that strand people. I'm talking about people who enter the wilderness and are unaware, unprepared, or incapable of basic skills. I spent a career responding to emergency situations to which I didn't know what I would encounter. Many an alarm was a test of preparedness. Being in the wilderness is no different.

My hope is that by reading this book, and heeding some of its advice, your trip will be uneventful except for the thrills one hopes: sunshine, great fishing, placid lakes, beautiful sunsets, and the joy of great company.

Let me finish by saying that if you have never been to the Boundary Waters and you enjoy rustic or wilderness camping, you need to experience this area. This type of experience is one that can only be enjoyed up close.

Chapter One

Getting Acquainted With the Area

The Boundary Waters Canoe Area Wilderness is located within the Superior National Forest in the northeast tip of Minnesota. This area is known as the Arrowhead Region, for obvious reasons when you see it on the map. Just north of the Boundary Waters, in the Ontario Province of Canada, is Quetico Provincial Park. Collectively this area is referred to as "Quetico-Superior," "canoe country," or simple the "boundary waters."

For the duration of this book, I shall refer to the Boundary Waters Canoe Area Wilderness as the Boundary Waters, Quetico Provincial Park as the Quetico, and the region collectively as the Boundary Waters area.

Superior National Forest and Quetico Provincial Park are bordered on the south and east by Lake Superior and Provincial Parks, to the south and west by the Mesabi Iron Range, Lake Vermillion, numerous state forests, and Voyageurs National Park, and to the north by the expanse of northern Ontario.

Larger cities in the area include Duluth, Minnesota/Superior, Wisconsin, to the south, International Falls, Minnesota/Fort Francis,

Ontario, Canada, to the west, and Grand Portage, Minnesota, and Thunder Bay, Ontario, Canada, to the east. Smaller Minnesota communities that directly supply goods and services to travelers to the Boundary Waters area include Two Harbors, Tofte, Grand Marais, Virginia, and Crane Lake. But most importantly you will want to be familiar with Ely, Minnesota, which is in the heart of the Superior National Forest and hence the Boundary Waters. In Canada locate Atikokan, Ontario, which sits just north of Quetico Provincial Park. Both of these cities provide goods, services, and lodging for travelers to the Boundary Waters area.

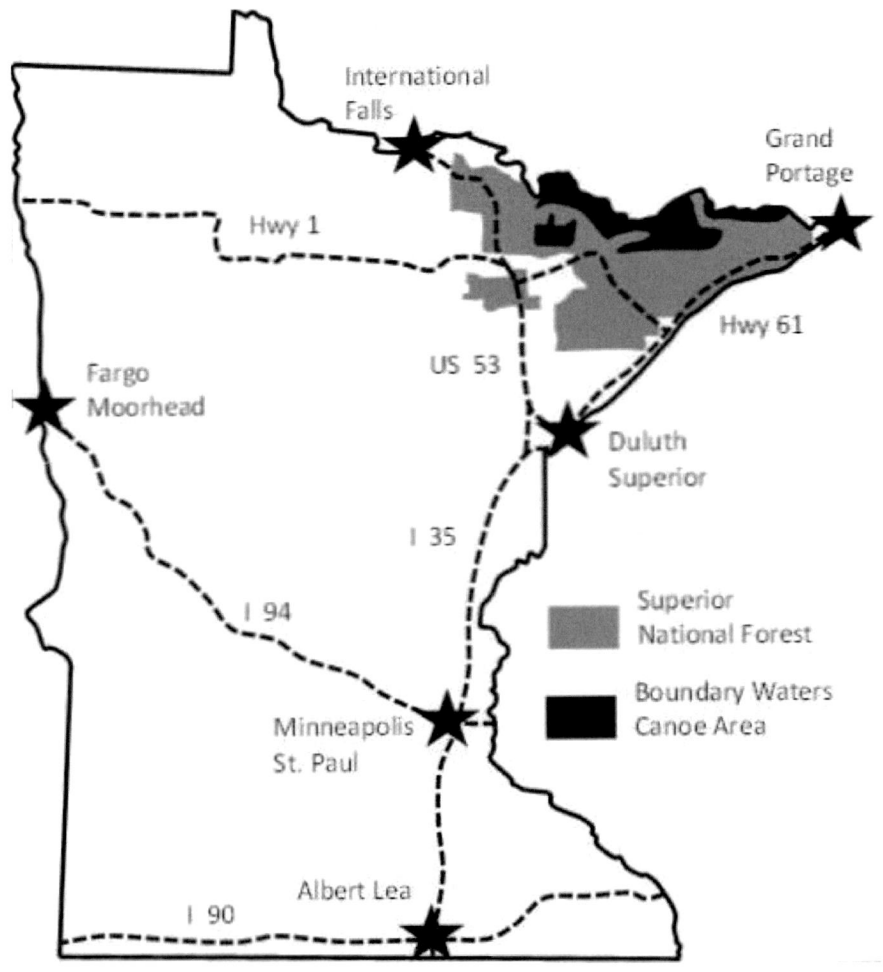

Geology

The Canadian Shield, or Laurentian Plateau, is a u-shaped region of exposed Precambrian igneous (volcanic) and metamorphic (physically/chemically changed) rock. The Precambrian time is the earliest of the geological ages starting about 4.5 billion years ago and ending about 540 million years ago. Precambrian time represents about 88 percent of earth's history. The shield covers most of east and central Canada, and reaches south into the United States as the Adirondack Mountains, Michigan's Upper Peninsula, northern Wisconsin, and the Superior Highlands, including the Boundary Waters area of northeast Minnesota. The Canadian Shield is one of the largest exposed rock formations on earth.

The shield was the first region of North America to be permanently elevated above sea level. This plateau was an area of active volcanos and mountains reaching as high as 39,000 feet above sea level. Over hundreds of millions of years these "mountains" have been reduced by erosion and glacial activity. Intermixed with this rock is a thin layer of top soil supporting forest growth but not well suited for agriculture.

A bonus to all of this exposed bedrock is easier access to mineral ore deposits. As a result, the Canadian Shield region holds some of the world's richest deposits of iron, copper, nickel, gold, and silver ore. Minnesota is the largest producer of iron ore and taconite (a lower grade iron ore) in the United States.

The Duluth Complex is part of the volcanic, mid-continent rift that pushed into the area about 1.1 billion years ago. It consists of various volcanic rocks, primarily gabbro. The Complex forms an arch from Duluth north to South Kawishiwi River, Gabbro Lake northeast to Knife Lake, then east along the Canadian border to Pigeon Point on Lake Superior. This Complex separates the Gunflint Iron Range from the Mesabi Iron Range, which is believed to have been one range prior to the rift pushing in.

Laurentide Ice Sheet

Numerous ice ages have occurred in earth's history. About 2.6 million years ago, the last ice age began. The latest glacial period of this ice age started about 1 million years ago and ended about 15,000 years ago. Most of Canada and the Great Lakes region of the United States were covered by the Laurentide Ice Sheet. The ice sheet was as thick as two miles in its northern reaches. In the Boundary Waters area, it was "only" a few thousand feet thick.

The ice sheet changed the exposed rocks by washing and scouring away the softer rocks leaving the harder bedrock. The size and shape of most of the lakes is due to this erosion and ancient fault lines. The ice sheet also deposited debris in areas forming moraines (hills and ridges). As the ice sheet melted and receded eskers (ridges) and kettles (large potholes) formed. In addition, the sheer weight of the ice sheet depressed the land surface as much as 2,000 feet. The result of all of this is thousands of lakes, rivers, and streams.

The shield is largely undeveloped, with boreal forest in the south and tundra to the north. The Boundary Waters area was once covered by a virgin forest consisting of large white pines. Today very little virgin timber remains. The forest now consists of aspen, birch, cedar, fir, maple, and pine. It is home to dozens of bird species including the common loon and the bald eagle. Moose and beavers are commonly sighted along with fewer sightings of otters, wolves, and black bears. It is also a fishing destination for many. Walleye, bass, pike, and trout are all here if you can catch them.

Eagle Mountain, located in the Misquah Hills in the Superior National Forest, southeast of Brule Lake, is the highest point in Minnesota at 2,301 feet. The lowest point in Minnesota is the Lake Superior shoreline.

Continental Divides

When most people hear "continental divide," they think of the Great Divide that bisects North America. In fact there are six divides that form watersheds, or basins, in North America.

The Laurentian Divide, which runs through northern Minnesota, divides the direction of waterflow in eastern and southern Canada and the upper midwestern United States. The northeast end of the divide is where the Labrador Sea meets the Hudson Strait. It travels south and west through eastern Canada.

The divide enters the United States in northeast Minnesota at the Height of Land Portage located in the Boundary Waters between North Lake and South Lake, just east of Gunflint Lake. The divide continues southwest through Minnesota. Near Hibbing it intersects with the St. Lawrence Divide at the Hill of Three Waters to form a three-way divide. The divide continues west across Minnesota, South Dakota, North Dakota, then re-enters Canada and crosses parts of Saskatchewan and Alberta. The divide drops back into the United States in Montana where it intersects with the Great Divide at Triple Divide Peak in Glacier National Park. The divide formed the northern boundary of the United States' Louisiana Purchase.

In the section of the divide that is within the Boundary Waters area, water north of the divide flows to the Arctic Ocean by way of the Rainy River and Winnipeg River systems, and on to Hudson Bay. Areas south of the Laurentian Divide and east of the St. Lawrence Divide flow to the Atlantic Ocean by way of the Great Lakes and through the St. Lawrence River system. Though not in the Boundary Waters area, drainage to the south of the Lauretian Divide and west of the St. Lawrence Divide flow to the Mississippi River or Missouri River systems and on to the Gulf of Mexico.

History

The first human inhabitants of the area are believed to have arrived around 8000 BCE. It is thought they came into the area following the receding glaciers and herds of large game. Around 3500 BCE, natives began fashioning tools and weapons from copper. In 1800 BCE, the natives are identified as that of the woodland culture of hunter gatherers. Both the Cree and the Dakota Sioux are known to have inhabited the area. Around 1000 AD, the birch bark canoe was introduced, replacing the dugout canoe. The birch bark canoe is much lighter and more maneuverable, allowing for greater travel. The first European explorers met both the Cree and Dakotas.

The Cree eventually moved west to the Plains. At about the same time, the Ojibwe of the Chippewa People started migrating in from the east. Tension between the Ojibwe and the Dakotas persisted until 1679 when a peace treaty was established with the help of Daniel Greysolon, Sieur du Lhut, the namesake of the City of Duluth. The Ojibwe eventually became the dominant tribe in the area by driving the Dakota to the south and west.

In 1782-1783, a smallpox epidemic decimated the native tribes. Some history recitations indicate the transfer of small pox to the natives was done deliberately, however there is no evidence of this being done in the Boundary Waters area. The natives were an intricate part of the fur trade.

The natives also were critical in the exploration of this region. When we mention the European explorers, be reminded that in most cases they were led by a native guide through established native trails.

Governing Bodies

In 1534, Jacques Cartier planted a cross in Gaspe Bay on the south shore of the St. Lawrence River and claimed the land for France. New France was born.

The Treaty of Utrecht was signed in 1713 and brought an end to what was known as Queen Anne's War in America and the War of the Spanish Succession in Europe (1701-1714). As a result, France ceded to Britain any claims to Hudson Bay and its tributaries (Rupert's Land) including the Boundary Waters area north of the Laurentian Divide.

Following the signing of the Treaty of Paris (1763), Britain gained control of the remainder of what would become Canada. The treaty ended the war between Britain and France commonly referred to as the French and Indian War in America and the Seven Years' War in Europe (1756-1763).

The United States gained control of the southern Great Lakes region after the American Revolutionary War (1775-1783). Britain maintained control of British North America (Canada). Areas above and east of the Mississippi River and east of Lake of the Woods became part of the United States' Northwest Territory. Areas to the west of the Mississippi were part of France's Louisiana Territory.

During this time the border between the United States and British North America remained unclear. Britain believed the border followed the waterways from Fond du Lac (Duluth) north via the St. Louis River, among others, to Rainy Lake. The United States believed the border to be from Fort William (Thunder Bay) west via the Kaministiquia River, among others, to Rainy Lake. The disputed area encompassed most of the Boundary Waters area.

This dispute continued until 1842 when the Webster-Ashburton Treaty established the border as the "waterways from Grand Portage west by way of the Pigeon River, among others, to Rainy Lake, and on to Lake of the Woods, following the traditional trade route." This is the border we recognize today.

The Louisiana Purchase of 1803 brought the Mississippi and the Missouri rivers and their tributaries under United States' control. This includes the remainder of the current state of Minnesota. The Convention of 1818 established the boundary between the United States and British North America as the 49th Parallel from Lake of the Woods to the Rocky Mountains.

In 1854, the Treaty of La Pointe is signed by the Chippewa Indian Peace Commission, ceding the land in the Arrowhead Region to the United States. This opened the area up to settlers and prospectors.

As new states are formed in the United States, territories are renamed. The Boundary Waters area started as a part of the Northwest Territory and then became a part of the Indiana Territory in 1800, Illinois Territory in 1809, Michigan Territory in 1818, Wisconsin Territory in 1836, and the Minnesota Territory in 1849.

In 1858, the east side of the Minnesota Territory becomes the United States' thirty-second state, Minnesota. The western half becomes part of the Dakota Territory.

Exploration by Europeans

In 1660, Medard Chouart des Groseilliers and Pierre-Esprit Radisson explored the north shore of Lake Superior. This is the first documented exploration of the region. Some believe the area may have been visited as early as 1362 by Scandinavian explorers. The belief is based on the Kensington Rune Stone found near Kensington, Minnesota, in 1898. Most archeologists say the stone is a hoax.

In 1688-1689, Jacques de Noyan and native guides traveled what will be called "the traditional route" from Grand Portage on Lake Superior to Rainy Lake. He wintered in the Rainy Lake area. In 1731, Pierre Gaultier de Varennes, sieur de La Verendrye and his four sons begin exploration west of Lake Superior. They establish Fort St. Pierre on Rainy Lake in 1731, Fort St. Charles on Lake of the Woods in 1732, and Fort Maurepas on the south end of Lake Winnipeg in 1734.

Alexander Mackenzie, a *coureur des bois* (agent) for the North West Company, continued exploration further west. In 1789 he reached the Arctic Ocean by way of the Dene River, among others. The river was renamed the Mackenzie River in his honor. Three years later he traveled by way of the Peace River, among others, to the Pacific Ocean.

In 1797, David Thompson, a mapmaker for the North West Company who would become the greatest mapmaker of North America, produced the first good maps of the area.

The Fur Trade

In 1670, the Hudson's Bay Company is formed and licensed to trade in North America. A trading post is established at York Factory on Hudson Bay to trade with the natives for fur. The area they are licensed to operate in is the Hudson Bay area and its tributaries, including the Boundary Waters area north of the Laurentian Divide. This area is known as Rupert's Land after Prince Rupert, the first governor of the Hudson's Bay Company. The Hudson's Bay Company is still in business today and is the oldest company in North America.

By the 1690s, the French *coureurs des bois* were sent to live with and establish trade agreements with the natives. A coureur des bois would trade furs for European goods such as cloth, wool, tools, firearms, ammunition, gunpowder, and liquor.

In 1779, the North West Company is organized and headquartered in Montreal with a trade depot at Grand Portage. They compete directly with the Hudson's Bay Company and numerous skirmishes between them were recorded. The North West Company set up a vast network of ninety-seven forts, or trading posts, stretching all the way to the Rocky Mountains. The fur trade was at its peak during this time. The voyageurs (travelers) used large boats called *bateaus* to transport the trade goods from Montreal to Grand Portage and return with the furs.

These boats were as big as ten feet by fifty feet. The primary means of propulsion was by paddle but some of the larger boats had small sails.

For the inland waters west of Grand Portage, they would use a "north canoe." These canoes were about four feet by twenty-four feet and could haul six voyageurs and thirty 90-pound packs for a 500-mile journey

The American Fur Company began operations in 1808. By this time, the Hudson's Bay Company and the North West Company had established their networks of trading posts and agents in the Boundary Waters area and west. The American Fur Company focused its operations in the United States and its territories. They established trading posts in the southern Great Lakes, along the Missouri River, the Rocky Mountains, and the Pacific Northwest, establishing a trading post in Astoria, Washington, in 1811. It also established commercial fishing villages in the Great Lakes, including one at Grand Marais from 1823 to 1840. The American Fur Company would go on to become one of the richest companies in America.

The competition between the two British fur companies continued and culminated in 1816 with the Battle of Seven Oaks along the Red River in Manitoba. Twenty-two people were killed in the battle. Pressure from the British government, because of the hostilities between the rival companies, led to a merger of the companies in 1821.

The fur trade started to decline in the early 1800s. Overharvesting, the War of 1812, and a change in European hat styles led to the end of the era in the early 1840s. After these companies left the area, a European presence remained with trading posts at Grand Portage and Superior.

European Settlement

When the Treaty of La Pointe was signed in 1854, numerous land claims were made in the Arrowhead Region. Mining made up the bulk of those claims. Most were abandoned by 1857 due to a financial panic that left little money for investment. By 1858, settlements were reported at Duluth, Superior, French River, Buchanan, Knife River, Agate Bay, Burlington Bay (in 1885 Agate Bay and Burlington Bay became Two Harbors), Stewart River, Silver Creek, and Grand Portage. Small amounts of gold were discovered in 1865 near Vermilion Lake, prompting a gold rush.

The rush was over by 1867, but it brought new settlers back into the region and was the impetus behind the building of the Vermilion Trail. This trail extended from Duluth to Vermilion Lake, following Dakota and Ojibwe trails. Today, County Highway 4 and State Highway 135 follow the same path.

In 1869, the railroad from St. Paul reached Duluth. At the start of the year the population of Duluth was barely 100 people. By the end of the year, it was more than 3,000. With another financial panic in 1873, half of the people left. But with the increase in mining activity in the 1880s, they returned and the towns grew to become major ore and grain shipping ports.

In the 1870s commercial fishing villages were established at Beaver Bay, Tofte, Lutsen, and Grand Marais. These villages were supplied by "collection steamers" from Duluth. These steamers ferried goods to the villages and returned to Duluth with fish that had been caught. Commercial fishing in the region flourished until the 1930s.

During this time, roads were being built as settlers pushed northward and inland. A wagon trail along the shoreline from Duluth was started and finally made its way to Grand Portage in 1880. By 1926 this trail was improved to allow for motor-vehicle traffic. This road became U.S. Highway 61, though it wasn't paved until 1933.

The Gunflint Trail, a road leading towards the Gunflint Iron Range from Grand Marais, was started in the 1870s. It eventually made its way to Saganaga Lake by the 1930s, the Civilian Conservation Corp helping make it possible. In 1898 the Sawbill Trail was started between Tofte and Sawbill Lake. It was completed in 1931.

Improvements to these roads also allowed for greater transportation of goods. Fish was now hauled cheaper by truck rather than steamer. But with the roads came the tourists. As the roads improved and the fisheries declined, many residents built cabins and offered guide services. Tourism started to become an industry by the 1930s.

Fishing and mining were the primary calling to the area but some farming was done. Because of the Canadian Shield, the area makes for poor farming in the region. Most settlers maintained sustenance gardens and feed crops for themselves and their animals.

As the mining industry increased, railroads were built to haul the ore. In 1884, a railroad was built from Tower to the new ore docks at Agate Bay, soon to be Two Harbors. This line serviced the Vermilion Iron Range. In 1889, a rail was extended from Duluth to Two Harbors, and in 1892, a rail was laid to Mountain Iron to service the Mesabi Iron Range. Many more spurs were added to accommodate both the mining and logging industries.

As mining and logging in the region declined, so did the population. Many settlements, mines, and rails were abandoned. The regions industrial peak was from the 1880s to the 1950s. The 1890s saw the largest population of the region, greater than it is today.

Mining

Prospectors began looking for valuable minerals, primarily gold, shortly after the Treaty of La Pointe was signed. It had been rumored by Indian agents, explorers, and voyageurs that gold, silver, copper, and iron could be found.

In 1865, what would become the Vermilion Iron Range was discovered. The range is located between Tower and Ely. At first it was mined for gold during the Vermilion Lake Gold Rush. Hardly any gold was found. What was found was embedded in quartz, and not profitable to mine. The gold claims were abandoned by 1867. Iron mining began in 1882 and the first shipments went out in 1884 when the railroad arrived.

The range contained deeper veins of iron ore requiring vertical shafts and underground operations. Mining continued in the area until 1962, when the Soudan Mine in Tower was closed, and in 1967, when the Pioneer Mine in Ely was closed. The Soudan Mine is open for tours, including the underground operations.

Iron ore was discovered near Gunflint Lake in the 1850s. Due to access and the economy, exploratory shafts were not started until 1888. In 1891 mining operations were started on the Paulson Mine, but the first ore was not shipped out until 1892 when the railroad arrived. This area was referred to as the Gunflint Iron Range and extended northeast into Canada. Gun Flint City was built nearby. Operations ceased in 1893 because of financial reasons and the mine and city was abandoned. You can visit this area by hiking the Centennial Trail west of Gunflint Lake. The water-filled vertical shaft is still there with some exploratory shafts and mining debris.

The Mesabi Iron Range was discovered around 1866 and mining operations started at the Mountain Iron Mine in 1890. The Biwabik followed in 1891. The first shipments went out when the railroad arrived at Mountain Iron in 1892. It is the largest of the ranges extending from Grand Rapids to Babbitt. The iron ore in this range is close to the surface so open-pit mining is possible.

In the early 1890s, there were more than 100 mining companies. The iron mines became very successful and, as the mines grew, towns had to be relocated: Eveleth in 1900; Sparta, which was renamed Gilbert, in 1909; and Hibbing in 1919. The Hull-Rust-Mahoning Mine in Hibbing is the largest open-pit, iron-ore mine in the world and is open for viewing. Over the years mining operations have consolidated. Today six mining companies continue operations, primarily for taconite, a low-grade ore requiring processing to extract the iron.

The Cuyuna Iron Range was the last of the ranges to open. Discovered around 1904, mining operations did not start until 1911. It is located between Brainerd and Aitkin. As in the Vermilion Range, the ore veins run deeper requiring underground mining. At its peak twenty-seven mines were being worked. It is also known for Minnesota's worst mining accident, the Milford Mine Disaster, in 1924. Blasting too close to a lake resulted in flooding of the mine shaft, killing forty-one miners. Operations ended in 1984.

Once the ore was mined, it was hauled by rail to the ore docks at Two Harbors, Superior, or Duluth. The ore was loaded onto ships for transport to steel mills in Pittsburg, Gary, and others. Over the years the size of the ore docks has grown to keep up with the growth of the lake ships, commonly referred to as "lakers." Originally transported in barrels on the decks of schooners, the ships are now capable of hauling 70,000 tons of ore. The docks are uniform in size to meet the size and configuration of the lakers. Typically they are eighty feet high, sixty feet wide and range from 900 feet to 2,400 feet long. Examples are easily seen in the Duluth/Superior Harbor.

Logging

Commercial logging in the Boundary Waters area did not start right away do to the focus on mining and the cost of getting the lumber to markets. Active logging in Wisconsin, upper Michigan, and southern Minnesota were able to meet demands at a lower cost. In the 1850s, sawmills opened in Duluth and Beaver Bay to provide lumber for local use.

Soon, mills in Duluth and Superior grew dramatically due to their proximity to northern Wisconsin and southern Minnesota logging operations and their ability to ship product out of the twin ports. In the 1870s, trees were starting to be cleared along the Lake Superior shore. As these areas were cleared, loggers started pushing inland. By the 1890s, they had reached the Boundary Waters area. In 1895, logging camps were set up near Trout Lake, west of Ely. The railroad was used in some areas to haul out the logs. The rivers along the lake shore were also used to transport logs. Loggers would float the logs down to the lake shore, chain them together in large rafts, and tow them to the mills.

Logging increased, and by the 1930s the area was mostly clear of its virgin pine. As the canopy of these pines was removed, it allowed for the growth of spruce, balsam, cedar, aspen, and birch. In the 1930s, logging focused on these trees to supply pulpwood. Regulated logging continued in the Boundary Waters area until 1979 when the U.S. Forest Service prohibited logging in the wilderness area.

Superior National Forest

Superior National Forest first got its start in 1902 when 500,000 acres of forest land was set aside and protected from mining, homesteading, and unregulated logging. Additional acreage was set aside in 1905 and 1908. Steps were soon taken to have these three areas, totaling 1,018,638 acres, designated as National Forest. In February 1909, it was formally approved and the Superior National Forest was born. The Weeks Act of 1911 allowed for the purchase of private property by the federal government for inclusion into the forest. Land purchases were made in 1912, 1927, and an additional four purchases through the 1930s to bring the forest near its present size.

In 1925, seven hydroelectric dams were proposed in the area that would affect the water levels of the Boundary Waters area. As a result, the Shipstead-Newton-Nolan Act was passed in 1930 prohibiting land sale, alteration of natural water levels, and logging within 400 feet of shorelines in order to preserve the wilderness nature of these shorelines.

The Quetico Superior Committee was created in 1934 to advise the various federal agencies that governed the Superior National Forest.

From 1933-1942, the Civilian Conservation Corp set up fourteen camps in or near the Forest. Thousands of men were employed to plant trees, improve portages, build lookout towers, fight fires, and undertake numerous conservation projects.

The Thye-Blatnik Act of 1948 directed the purchase of the remaining resorts, cabins, and private lands within the Forest.

Large purchases were made in 1948, 1956, and 1961.

Today, the forest covers 3.9 million acres of forested lands. This includes 2,000 lakes and more than 3,400 miles of rivers and streams, for a total of almost half a million acres of water. Outside of the Boundary Waters, the Forest Service maintains access to seventy-seven lakes, twenty-two picnic areas, 2,000 miles of trails, twenty-three "fee campgrounds," seventeen "rustic campgrounds," and more than 270 "backcountry campsites." In addition, there is "dispersed camping" throughout the Forest. Restrictions apply to all types of camping, so check with the Forest Service before you go.

The Boundary Waters area, due to forward thinking people, has become a destination for tourists. Everyone tends to focus on the canoe area, which by itself is worth the trip, but there are a multitude of other attractions in the region. There is more information on these attractions in Chapter Ten.

Boundary Waters Canoe Area Wilderness

The Boundary Waters Canoe Area Wilderness is located within the Superior National Forest. It occupies more than a million of the Superior National Forest's 3.9 million acres. In 1921, Arthur Carhart, a recreational engineer with the Forest Service, wrote *Recreation Plans: Superior National Forest.* In his plan he wrote "we must allow our populace a communion with nature in areas of more or less wilderness conditions." He went on to propose canoe routes, portages, and campsites.

As a result, the Superior Roadless Area was created in 1926 with 640,000 acres of the Forest. It allowed for the construction of the Echo Trail, Fernberg Road, and the completion of the Gunflint Trail. The first policy statement for the Roadless Area contained these provisions:

- Retain as much wilderness as possible.
- Build no roads.
- Build simple campground facilities.
- Utilize careful methods of timber cutting.

The Little Indian Sioux River and Caribou Lake areas were added in 1939. The area was renamed the Superior Roadless Primitive Area. In 1951, private planes were prohibited from flying below 4,000 feet over the area. The name was again changed in 1958 to the Boundary Waters Canoe Area.

Probably the most definitive action to create the area as we know it was in 1964 with the signing of the Wilderness Act. This Act had a large impact in the preservation of "wilderness" forest land. Some of its provisions nationwide were:
- Created the National Wilderness Preservation System.
- Defined wilderness as: "A wilderness, in contrast with those areas where man and his own works dominate the landscape, is hereby recognized as an area where the earth and its community of life are untrammeled by man, where man himself is a visitor who does not remain."
- Set aside 9.1 million acres of National Forest as wilderness.
- Banned "motorized or mechanical vehicles or equipment" in these areas.
- Designated the Boundary Waters Canoe Area (BWCA) as a part of this wilderness system.

The BWCA was the only designated area with major exceptions to these provisions. These exceptions included logging and mining and the use of motorboats and snowmobiles. Numerous lawsuits were filed.

All of this controversy resulted in the Boundary Waters Canoe Area Wilderness Act of 1978. This Act added 50,000 acres to the wilderness area and changed its name to the Boundary Waters Canoe Area Wilderness. But most importantly it reinforced the wilderness nature of the area and placed restrictions on motorboats, snowmobiles, logging, and mining. Today, 109.5 million acres in 757 designated areas have been preserved as wilderness nationwide.
- Motorboats are prohibited in the Boundary Waters except on designated lakes, about 25 percent of the total Boundary Waters.
- Snowmobiles are prohibited in the Boundary Waters with some minor exceptions.

- Logging prohibited since 1979.
- Mining restricted to 222,000 acres along three corridors. The Secretary of Agriculture has the authority to acquire mineral rights.

Over the years, more rules were put in place. Some of the more common ones are:
- 1966, a permit system was started.
- 1971, cans and bottles prohibited.
- 1975, designated campsite usage for all areas.
- 1976, entry point quota system.
- 1981, reservation fee charged.
- 1994, group size limited to four canoes and nine people.

The Boundary Waters has 150 border miles with Canada, more than 2,000 designated campsites, twelve hiking trails, and 1,500 miles of canoe routes, with more than 1,000 lakes, rivers, and streams. The Boundary Waters sees more than 250,000 visitors, totaling more than 1 million visitor days, each year.

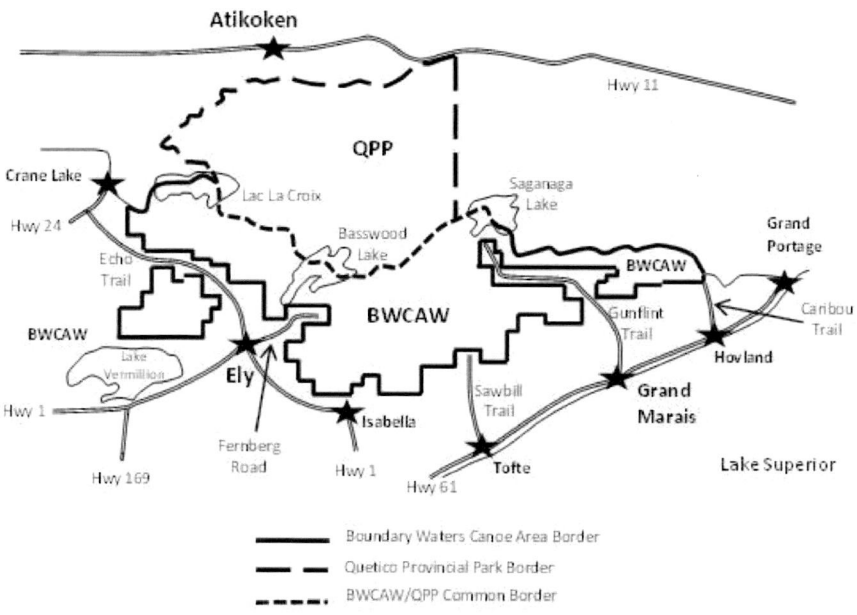

Quetico Provincial Park

Quetico Provincial Park was initially created as a way to regulate abusive hunting practices. Canada and the United States began working together to protect this region. The United States established the Superior National Forest in February 1909. This was followed in April by Canada establishing the Quetico Forest Preserve. Both the Forest and Preserve still allowed regulated trapping, hunting, fishing, and logging. The Provincial Parks Act created Quetico Provincial Park in 1913.

In 1915, the Lac La Croix First Nation was removed from their reserve within the Quetico boundaries. A grievance was filed, but it was not resolved until 1991. The settlement allowed the band to operate motorboats for guiding purposes in the area of their former reserve.

As with the Boundary Waters, the Quetico evolved.
- 1945, no more leases for private development.
- 1954, no private planes can be flown over the Quetico.
- 1954, Atikokan Highway opened (Trans-Canada Highway 11), allowing better access to the park.
- 1973, full wilderness protection granted; no logging or snowmobiles within the Quetico.
- 1979, motor vehicles and motorboats banned from the Quetico, with the Lac La Croix exception.
- 1976, cans and bottles prohibited.
- 2008, barbless hooks and nonorganic bait only for fishing.

The Quetico occupies more than 1.2 million acres of forested lands. It has more than 500 lakes and more than 2,000 unofficial campsites. More than 25,000 back-country visitors come each year. The Quetico and the Boundary Waters are similar in their access, use, and regulations for camping. The Quetico is in Canada and, therefore, requires special permits and documentation to enter. Access can be made from Canada or from the United States by passing through the Boundary Waters.

Chapter Two

Before You Go

I believe the enjoyment you get from the wilderness starts with your attitude. You are not going to a waterpark. It will not be warm and sunny every day. The bugs will bite. And challenges will be thrown at you.

The Boundary Waters area is a wilderness, you are a visitor, and you will be out of your element. Water, topography, weather, wind, animals, and fire rule the days and nights. Think through your trip and imagine what could happen. Are you ready for it? Be sure to pack the gear that you will need to meet these challenges and know how to use it. Have a good itinerary. Study your maps and learn the terrain.

Having the mindset and being prepared to meet these challenges is all part of the experience. Use caution and think through the problem before you act. At the end of the day you can look back on your accomplishments with pride.

Personal Health and Physical Condition

The remoteness of the Boundary Waters area puts some restrictions on who can venture into the wilderness. Your personal health and physical condition will determine what type of trip you can take. If you have any serious medical conditions, I would consider this area as a no-go. There is no 911, EMS, or hospitals that can get to you quickly, or you to them. If you have minor medical issues that are controlled, there is no reason for you not to go. Just be sure to bring any medications you will need and let your travel partners know of your condition(s).

Wilderness camping can be arduous. The terrain on portages is uneven and rock strewn and may contain some big elevation changes. Canoes weigh forty-five to sixty-five pounds and are cumbersome. Some people are uncomfortable sitting in a canoe daily for hours. And you may have to do all of this in inclement weather. If you are not in good physical condition, consider a less active, shorter-distance trip. You can find a lot of nice lakes just a few hours into the Boundary Waters. But, the closer you are to the entry points, the more people you will see.

Or you can get in shape. Start with stretching or yoga. You can do it at home or join a club. Start walking a few miles a day. Add a backpack with ten to twenty pounds in it gradually increasing the weight to forty-five pounds. Do this for a few months and it will make your time in the wilderness more enjoyable.

Remember that if you get hurt or have a medical problem, the burden of getting you out rests with the group with whom you are traveling. A simple sprained ankle may mean that someone now has to carry you or your pack over the portages and out of the wilderness.

Camping

Experience is hard to beat. You can read or watch how to be a wilderness camper, but having been there and done that is best. I will assume that anyone wanting to venture into the wilderness has some experience camping. If your experience is limited, I suggest going to a county or state park or forest. Many offer isolated sites. Some even have walk-in sites.

Superior National Forest is a good example of this type of camping. Use the same equipment to set up your camp as you would in the wilderness. Do all of your cooking and camp activities as if you were in the wilderness. Play with different ways of setting up your rain tarp or starting your campfire. Experiment with different camp recipes. Bake a dessert or bannock (pan) bread over the fire.

A good introduction to the area is to camp at one of the campsites in the Superior National Forest and take day trips into the Boundary Waters. Another option is to take short camping trips on the entry-point lakes. Both are good ways of getting your feet wet, literally. The Superior National Forest has forty campsites that have access to the lakes and rivers of the Boundary Waters.

Canoeing

Knowing how to handle a canoe is vital. The canoe is your vehicle once you enter the Boundary Waters. You would not jump behind the wheel of your car without some training. Treat your canoe the same. If you are not an experienced paddler, you need to get some time on the water before you go. I suggest you read a book and practice, or take canoeing lessons. Many of the sporting goods stores will be able to help you. If you do not have a canoe, borrow or rent one for the day. Grab your partner and head down to your local lake or pond.

The following are some basic exercises you can use to become familiar with the canoe:

Place the canoe on the ground. Do not sit or stand in a canoe that isn't floating. This will damage the hull. Look at the canoe seats. Imagine yourself sitting in the seat. The direction you are facing is the front or bow. Behind you is the back or stern. The top edges are called the gunwales (pronounced gunnel). The braces that go across are called thwarts. Crossing near the middle of the canoe is the portage yoke. If the canoe you are practicing with doesn't have a portage yoke, don't worry; you can practice getting the canoe over your head and carrying it later. But you will need a yoke for portaging.

Put the boat in the water, put on your personal flotation device, and grab a paddle. Now is a good time to get your feet wet. Proper loading and unloading of the canoe is done with it completely in the water. You may get lucky at some portages with well-placed rocks, but most of the time you will have wet feet. Even the portages themselves may be wet due to a recent rain, being in a low area, or beaver ponds.

Decide who will be in the front and who will be in the back. Carefully get in the canoe, keeping your weight centered in the boat. Have a seat and get comfortable. While near shore, grab the gunwales on both sides and rock the boat side to side. This will give you a feel for the boat's stability. It differs from one canoe to another. Grab your paddle. There are many ways of holding the paddle; to me it's whatever is comfortable. If you have a bent paddle, the tip of the blade, or bottom end, should bend to the front, the cup side of the blade toward the stern.

Find a landmark on the far shore in line with the bow. With just the bow paddler paddling, take your normal paddle stroke. Which way did the canoe go? Now do the same with the paddle on the other side. If you paddle on the left, you will push the boat forward and to the right. If you paddle on the right, you will push the boat forward and to the left.

Now turn your blade parallel to the gunwale, reach out – do not lean out – to the side and pull the paddle toward the canoe. As your paddle gets near the boat, rotate the blade a quarter turn and push it to the stern. Which way did you go? With practice you should be able to maintain a relatively straight course. This is called a "draw stroke." If you just do the draw part, you will be able to draw (pull) the boat, right side to the right, left side to the left. This stroke is not as powerful as your regular stroke, but you can control the boat from the front.

Do the same drill with just the stern paddler. Take your normal paddle stroke. Which way did the boat go? You will find it is the same as in the bow. If you paddle on the left, you will push the boat forward and to the right. If you paddle on the right, you will push the boat forward and to the left.

The next stroke to learn is the "J" stroke and is important for the stern paddler to know. Start with your normal stroke. As you near the end, rotate (pitch) the blade so it is parallel to the gunwale and gently push or pry the blade away from the boat. This rudder motion will compensate for any off-side push from your normal stroke, keeping you straight.

Moving across the water is easy if you work as a team. The bow paddler is primarily there for propulsion. The stern paddler adds propulsion and steering. When done correctly the paddles are on opposite sides of the boat. If you both paddle at the same time, you will cancel out each other's push and the canoe will follow a straight track. Every so often the stern paddler can use the "J" stroke to tweak your heading. When you start to tire, either paddler can call a "switch." Both paddlers then switch sides and, by doing so, you remain on opposite sides. Inexperienced paddlers are easy to spot. Their courses zigzag, wasting energy, and their paddles are waving in the air as they randomly switch from one side to the other.

These strokes will get you across open flat water. If you intend to do river trips, you need to learn more. If you intend to do any level of whitewater, you need to learn much more. In our canoes we give our stern paddlers the title "boat captain." Boat loading, navigating, and course are their responsibility. We switch off this position to give everyone the experience.

Canoeing on the Little Indian Sioux River

Carrying a Canoe

To properly carry (portage) the canoe, it needs to be up and on your shoulders. To do this, start with the canoe upright on the ground. Locate the thwart in front of the rear seat. If you are on the left side of the canoe, grab this thwart with your right hand near the gunwale. If you are on the right side, use your left hand. Face the canoe with your toes under the edge. Reach out and place your other hand on the same thwart near its middle. Now lean back as you lift/slide the stern of the canoe up on your thighs. The bow of the boat should stay on the ground. In this position you can bounce the canoe up by lifting your rear leg.

Now bounce and lift the canoe up over your head while sliding your hand from the middle of the thwart to the outside. With practice you will be able to do this in one motion. The bow of the boat should be pointed into the ground and the stern high in the air. Once overhead carefully move your hands to the gunwales. Walk your hands forward along the gunwales until you reach the portage yoke. Lower the canoe to your shoulders allowing the bow to come off the ground. Adjust the canoe so it is comfortable and the bow slightly raised for visibility. Reverse the procedure to gently place the canoe back on the ground.

Many a seasoned canoeist prefers to lift the canoe from the side without grounding the bow. They believe it lessens the wear and tear on the canoe. This is true, but for a novice who is not use to the weight and balance of a canoe, I feel the above-described method is safer. Add uneven terrain and wind, and it's an invitation to a strained back, sprained ankle, or a canoe bouncing on the rocks. If you are concerned with scratching the canoe, place a couple strips of duct tape on the bow tip to protect it.

Portaging the canoe

Tips:
- Point the bow in the direction you intend to travel before lifting.
- Make sure the bow is grounded in soft dirt/sand or butt it against a root or a rock.
- Check for overhead branches or other obstacles.

For short portages, use the two-person carry. Place your packs on your backs and carry the empty canoe with one person on one side at the bow and the other person on the other side at the stern. A canoe is designed so the water supports the weight of the load. This is the reason it's so light when unloaded. Do not carry a loaded canoe.

A canoe should be loaded while it is floating. Loading a canoe while it sits on shore may damage the canoe. Dragging a loaded canoe is bad. Yes, you may have to get your feet wet. Keeping the packs low in the canoe will also provide better stability. A properly loaded canoe is much more stable in the water and easier to handle.

Navigating

Once you enter the Boundary Waters, you need to be able to find your way around. Nothing is marked. Not the portages, not the campsites, nothing. The ability to navigate is a must. I am a proponent of the traditional map and compass method. I know about all the electronic gadgets that are available, but that is what I leave at home. Neither my compass nor my map have run out of battery power or lost a signal. Self-reliance is one of the reasons I go to the Boundary Waters, or any wilderness. Even if you do use electronic navigation, take along a map and compass and know how to use them in case there is a malfunction. Part of the fun is learning how to find your way around with just the map and compass.

By using a map and compass, you become more aware of your overall position. By noting landmarks on the map, you will be able to track your course easier. Mark islands, peninsulas, escarpments, even campsites and portages. You will learn to keep your head up and look for these landmarks as you travel and be more aware of your surroundings and location. When you navigate electronically, you tend to watch your device rather than the terrain.

A good map is essential. Without one you truly will be lost. Finding your way can sometimes be difficult even with one. Some of the lakes with islands, peninsulas, and bays can be challenging. To quote Daniel Boone, "No, I can't say I was ever lost, but I was bewildered once for three days."

The maps I have used are the Fisher and the McKenzie. I find the Fisher maps are easier to read the portages and campsites, whereas the McKenzie maps show the topography better. You can also go online to voyageurmaps.com. They have interactive maps that can help you in planning your trip. Or you can purchase any of these maps online, by mail, at most outfitters, or at some map stores. Check your local store and see what they carry. In Contacts / Resources at the back of the book is information you need for purchasing them online.

The next item you need is a compass. We are talking about magnetic compasses. You want one that is reliable. The bubble style, clip-on, knife-hilt mounted, or combination compass, whistle, and thermometer won't make it. It should have a clear base, rotating bezel, and orienting lines. You can go one better and get one that has a sight mirror and magnetic declination adjustment, but I haven't found them necessary where we go.

Magnetic Declination

Congratulations, you are going to one of the few spots on earth where magnetic declination matters little.

What is magnetic declination? There are two North Poles: the Geographic North Pole and the Magnetic North Pole. Compasses work by pointing to the Magnetic North Pole. Maps are oriented to the Geographic North Pole. These two poles are actually about 250 miles apart, and changing. It just so happens that in the Boundary Waters area, they almost line up.

The zero declination (agonic) line runs through International Falls, Minnesota, as of 2010. The western half of the boundary waters is about -1^0 whereas the eastern half is about -2^0. Not enough to worry about. If you head to either of the coasts of the United States, the declination varies +/- 15^0 to 18^0. Navigational maps should have the declination printed on them and you will have to add or subtract to determine Geographic North versus Magnetic North.

Using a Compass

Most of us have used a compass at some point in time. The red magnetic needle points to the north. I will leave out the simple north, south, east, west stuff.

To establish a bearing, hold the compass level in front of you and point the bearing (direction of travel) arrow in the direction you wish to go. Now turn the bezel so the red base arrow lines up with the red magnetic arrow. Your bearing, in degrees, will be the number on the bezel that lines up with the bearing arrow.

Once you have established your bearing, plot a landmark in your direction of travel and work toward it. If you lose sight of the landmark, use the compass. Hold the compass in front of you and ROTATE YOUR BODY until the red magnetic needle lines up with the red arrow on the base of the bezel. DO NOT twist the bezel.

The bearing arrow is now pointing in the direction you want to go. Next, learn how to transfer a bearing (direction of travel) from a map (map to compass). Plot or visualize your starting and destination points on a map. Place the compass on the map and line up one of the side edges of your compass baseplate with this line of travel. Be sure your "bearing arrow" on the baseplate is pointing in the direction of travel.

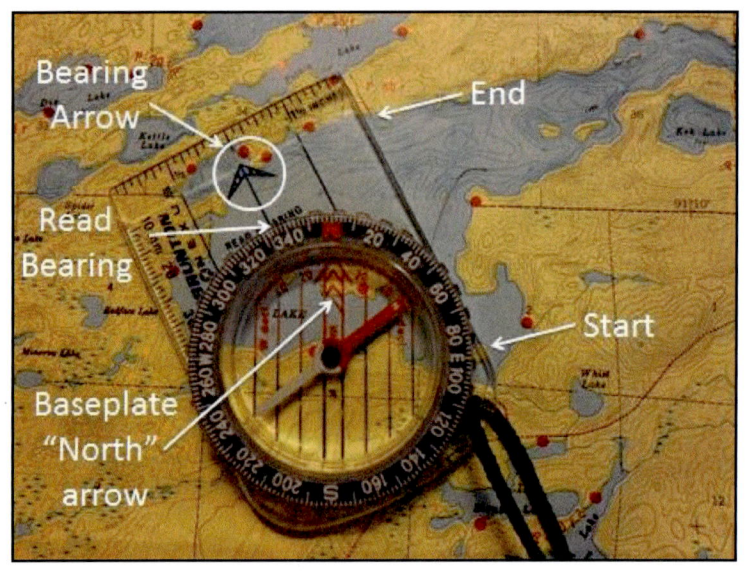

Transferring a bearing from a map to a compass

Now hold the baseplate and rotate the bezel so the red "North" arrow on the base of the bezel lines up with the north/south lines on the map. Your bearing, in degrees, will be the number on the bezel that lines up with the bearing arrow.

To follow this bearing, take the compass off the map. Hold the compass in your palm in front of you with the base plate level and the bearing arrow pointing away from you. Rotate your body until the red magnetic needle lines up with the red north arrow on the base of the bezel. The bearing arrow is now pointing in the direction you want to go.

Pick a landmark on the horizon or the other side of the lake that lines up with the bearing arrow. Walk or paddle to this point and repeat the process.

Navigating the seas and wilderness has been going on for millennia. Prior to reliable compasses or GPS, navigation was done using the sun, stars, and chronometers. The knowledge these early navigators possessed is inspiring. Today the same stars and sun are up there and our watches have become quite accurate. Navigating by this way is still possible. Using Polaris to locate north at night or a watch during the day is still valid. A canoe and paddle can be used as a sundial. Go online and look up some of the older methods and the next time you are in the wilderness give them a try. You might be surprised with the results.

First Aid and Medical Training

One of my biggest fears is that someone will get hurt. My years in the fire service and as a paramedic have proven that accidents do happen and people do get hurt. In the wilderness it is not possible to carry all the gear and have the proper training for every conceivable accident. But you should be equipped and be able to treat minor injuries and illnesses. Thus far we have not had anyone injured in our corps. But we have treated other canoeists for lacerations, sprains, and a probable fractured fibula.

When you are on vacation in the Boundary Waters area, you will be doing physical activity that you are not used to. Hauling gear over uneven terrain or paddling, using your upper body for hours a day, are not normal activities. Because of this, strains and sprains do happen. The best way to prevent this is to be in shape, pace yourself, don't overload yourself on portages, step carefully, and don't take chances. Jumping from rock to rock to avoid getting your feet wet is an invitation to a sprained ankle. And don't forget that when you are in camp, you will be playing with fire and sharp objects like saws and knives.

During every trip you can expect someone to have discomfort from bug bites, sunburn, aching muscles, and, possibly, blisters. The longer or more often you are in the wilderness, the better your chances are of seeing cuts, bruises, and burns. Occasionally you or one of your group may experience abdominal discomfort or diarrhea. This may be due to poor hygiene, not filtering or treating your water correctly, or the fajitas.

You will need to learn how to treat these illnesses or injuries. Everyone has some first-aid skills. Most are geared to the minor cuts and bruises everyone experiences. But how would you treat a severely sprained ankle or a deep laceration? As I stated earlier in this chapter, there is no 911. You are on your own. Various organizations offer first-aid training classes, including the Red Cross. I suggest at least two of you take a class. Until one of my sons became a paramedic, I was the only one with advanced first-aid skills. I often wondered what would happen if I were the one seriously hurt.

A first-aid kit is a must, even on the shortest trips. There are many preassembled kits available. Sit down and think of what could happen to you or your group. Make a list of the items you believe you will need to treat these illnesses or injuries, then find a kit similar to your list. You can always add to an existing kit or, if you don't find what you're looking for, create your own. Appendix 1 includes a list of the items my travel partners and I carry for our trips. Some might consider it a bit much, but when it comes to safety, I would rather have it and not need it, than need it and not have it.

When cleaning a wound, use a glove to protect the wound from your dirty hand. Do not use lake water, filtered or unfiltered, to clean the wound. Use antiseptic soap and flush with sterile water or saline. Apply some antibacterial cream and cover with a dressing. Normally you do not want to reduce, or pop, blisters. In the wilderness, you may have to for comfort. Then clean the wound as described above. Use mole skin or duct tape to prevent further damage. After a couple days, you can cut away the dead tissue to aid in healing.

Wildlife

One of the big attractions of being in the wilderness is the wildlife. Everyone enjoys catching a glimpse of a moose, a loon, or any other animal or bird you normally wouldn't see. But along with this comes the potential for confrontation. Remember that you are on their turf. There are rules that all wildlife play by to which we are clueless. Buy a book or manual to help you identify some of the lesser-known critters or birds. One of the biggest concerns I hear is the fear of wildlife. Below is a summary of some of the more common animals you may encounter and precautions you will want to take to protect yourself.

Black Bear

Let's start with the black bear. It seems most people have a preconceived fear of bears. Perhaps it's the teeth and claws. Much of this fear is because television and Hollywood portray them all as man-eaters. People have told me they won't go camping for fear of a bear tearing through their tent in the middle of the night. Others say they would only go if they can carry a sidearm. In all my years traveling in the wilderness, I have found this unnecessary. Yes, there have been occasions where bears have attacked, but it is not the norm. Investigations into the rare black bear attacks have shown most of the attacks were because the bear was cornered. If given the option, bears will beat a hasty retreat.

The black bear is the only bear in the Boundary Waters area. Black bears are not man-eaters. Their diet consists of grasses, berries, fruits, and a few little critters. This is not to say they are not opportunists. If you leave your food out, they will find it. Black bears have a keen sense of smell. They stand about two-and-a-half to three feet tall at the shoulder and weigh between 150 and 350 pounds. They truly are more afraid of you than you are of them. That is why they are not often seen.

Most encounters with bears occur at campsites. With food around they tend to get more curious and braver. Rarely do they become aggressive. The U.S. Forest Service lists these precautions you should take:
- Keep a clean campsite.
- Never eat or store food in your tent.
- Hang your food pack and garbage or place it in a bear-proof container. We will talk more about this in Chapter Seven.
- If a bear enters camp, shout, clap, bang pots, and throw rocks to scare it off.
- If a bear becomes aggressive, change campsites. Report the encounter to the Forest Service.

Bear encounters while traveling are not common. Usually it is a result of you being quiet and coming from a downwind direction. If a bear hears or smells you, they are usually gone before you get there. Travelers in brown and grizzly bear country will make noise while walking or carry noisemakers attached to their packs. If you have a phobia about bears, this also will work with black bears. If you encounter a black bear while on a portage or hike, follow these precautions.
- Give the bear room so it can retreat.
- Make noise, wave your arms, shout, and clap your hands.
- Do not run; stand your ground and move slowly away.

Moose

The next big animal you are likely to encounter is the moose. I am more concerned about meeting a moose than I am a bear. A healthy adult moose is the king/queen of the forest. Even wolves, the moose's only predator other than man, will shy away from them. We have encountered more moose than bear in the Boundary Waters area. Twice these encounters were way too close for my comfort.

Moose will grow to six feet high at the shoulder and weigh 1,000 to 1,200 pounds. Their diet is primarily water plants and twigs. They are likely to be spotted in emergent vegetation along lake shores or in river systems. Moose are good swimmers and may be spotted crossing rivers or lakes.

Moose are generally pretty laid back but will become aggressive if they feel threatened. Remember there are few things in the forest they fear. You are not one of them. They do not scare off easily. Move away and give them space. If you cannot move, find an object, a tree or a rock, to hide behind. If their ears lay back, they are likely to charge. Unlike a bear, it is OK to move away from a moose. Just remember they are capable of running 30 mph. If you spot a moose and keep your distance, it makes for a great experience and photo opportunity.

Chub River moose

White-Tailed Deer

White-tailed deer are common, grow to about three feet at the shoulder, and weigh from 150 to 250 pounds. They feed on a variety of vegetation including grasses, leaves, and small plants. Deer are shy. If you are noisy, you may not see any, or possibly only their white flag of a tail waving as they run away.

Wolf

The last of the larger animals you may see is the Timber Wolf. These wolves can grow to an average of two-and-a-half feet at the shoulder and weigh from 70 to 100 pounds. By the 1950s wolves had been hunted and trapped to near extinction in the lower forty-eight states. Since then they have been protected and have rebounded.

Their diet consists of bigger game such as deer and a young, old, or sickly moose. They supplement these meals with small game, berries, mice, and birds. Contrary to what you have seen on television, wolves are not a threat to humans. Wolves will avoid people and are very good at it. It is rare to see one in the wild. It is possible, and a rare treat, to hear them howling. In my wilderness travels, I have seen only three wolves: two in Michigan's Upper Peninsula and one in the Boundary Waters area. The Boundary Waters area holds the largest population of wolves in the lower forty-eight states.

Beaver

Occasionally you may see a beaver. Beaver are the largest rodent in North America. They grow to about three-and-a-half feet from nose to tail and they weigh from thirty-five to sixty pounds. Twigs and bark are their primary diet, with aspen being their favorite. Beaver are the primary reason this area was initially explored.

When swimming they have a distinct V-shaped wake. They are capable of swimming long distances underwater. Even if you don't see a beaver, you will surely see their handiwork. Lodges and dams are abundant, and you may even have the pleasure of wading through a beaver pond that has flooded part of a portage.

If you plan on traveling on any river system, the chances of running across a beaver dam are good. I find the construction and stability of these dams to be impressive. Long-established dams may have portages around them. For most of them, you will have to work your gear and canoe over them.

Otter

The river otter is another rare treat that is not often seen. I have never seen one out of the water in the wild. They can be very protective of their young, as I witnessed at Rum Lake. They can grow as long as four feet from nose to tail and weigh twenty pounds. Their diet consists of fish, crayfish, frogs, and clams.

Red Squirrel

The red squirrel is common. It is the critter that will greet you with its chatter when you walk into many campsites, and will continue to let you know whose turf you are on. They can grow to twelve inches from nose to tail. They eat nuts and seeds and will hoard spruce and pine cones for the long winter. In camp they will get into anything open and unguarded. Sunflower seeds and trail mix are favorites. And, as happened on Isle Royale, they are capable of chewing through a brand new backpack to get to them.

Chipmunk

Chipmunks are also common in camp. They will forage for anything dropped or left behind. They can grow to nine inches from nose to tail. They are also hoarders who feed on nuts, seeds, and plant buds. They can be brave and will come close to you in their pursuit of food. Trail mix and sunflower seeds are also their favorite.

Common Loon

I believe the loon, for most people, is the one thing they associate with the wild. The sight of a loon, or their call, lets people know they are truly in a remote area. Having a pair of loons serenade you in the evening is relaxing to me. The common Loon is the Minnesota state bird. It weighs about ten pounds and feeds on fish. It is an excellent swimmer and is capable of diving to more than 200 feet.

Common Loon

Merganser

Another water-based bird you may see is the Common Merganser. It is about the size of a Mallard duck. The female is easily recognizable by her back-flowing, reddish-brown crest. It has been referred to as a "Mohawk" or "punk" hairdo. She has a grey body with a white breast. The male has a green head, white body, and a red beak; no crest for him. Mergansers are fish eaters, diving for their meals. They nest in tree cavities dug out by woodpeckers. Mergansers are called "Sawbills" because of the serrations on the edge of their beaks for catching fish. The lake and trail got its name from these birds.

Bald Eagle

The Bald Eagle is the national bird and symbol of the United States. It appears on most of our money and on The Great Seal of the United States. It is the only eagle unique to North America. During the 1960s they were almost wiped out by pesticides that weakened their eggs. Since DDT was banned in 1972, eagles have rebounded and are a common sight in the Boundary Waters area.

They primarily eat fish but will supplement that with other birds and small animals. They are also known to scavenge food killed by others or steal food from smaller predators. They can grow to three feet long with wingspans of seven feet and weigh from ten to fourteen pounds. Immature Bald Eagles are often confused with Golden Eagles because of their brown plumage. They make large stick nests in the top of tall mature trees. It's hard to beat the grandeur of the Bald Eagle.

Turkey Vulture

Another large bird you may see soaring overhead is the Turkey Vulture. Turkey Vultures are black with a bald red head. From afar you may assume it is an eagle. I find the best way to recognize them from a distance is their small head and short neck. A mature eagle's head will stick out; a vulture's smaller, dark head does not. Turkey Vultures feed on dead animals (carrion) of all kinds. They have an excellent sense of smell and are masters at riding the thermals in search of a meal.

Insects

It seems everything good comes at a price. I think the price for the wilderness is the bugs. I know they are an integral part of the ecosystem, but I wish they would feed on someone else. Although bugs can be a nuisance, it's still not enough to outweigh the joy of being in the wilderness.

Mosquito

The mosquito is the scourge of the summer outdoors. If you are an active outdoors person, you already deal with them. From mid-May through August they reign. Most people are familiar with them so little needs to be said. They are most active at dawn and dusk. However, I believe they patiently wait at every portage for canoeists to land. Only the female bites as she needs the protein in blood for her egg production. This is common for all of these biting insects.

Black Fly

Few people who are out and about and near water in the summer don't know of the black fly. These are little pinhead-sized biting flies that primarily inhabit rivers and streams. They are active from mid-May through June. Because of their size, they are difficult to spot. Unlike a mosquito, you may not feel their bite, but you will soon notice a very itchy welt that may last for days.

Deer Fly

Another biting fly is the deer fly. Their bite is not as nasty as a black fly, but they are the ones who annoy you by buzzing around your head, getting into your hair, and trying to get up your nose and in your ears. They are about half an inch long with green or golden eyes.

Horse Fly

The last, but certainly not least, of the biting flies is the horse fly. They are dark-colored and about three-quarters of an inch long. They are well known for attacking your lower extremities. Unlike a black fly, you will feel it when a horse fly bites.

Ticks

The Boundary Waters area has both the wood tick and the deer tick, also called the black-legged tick. The wood tick is the larger of the two. The wood tick is about three-eighths of an inch in length and has a dark body with white markings. The deer tick is much smaller. It is about one-eighth of an inch in length and is orange-brown in color. Deer ticks carry Lyme disease.

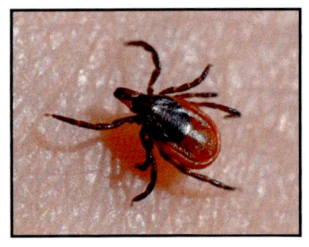

Deer tick

Ticks are primarily found in areas of tall grass or bushes. They also seem to be quite common around campsites. The Centers for Disease Control and Prevention (CDC) says that ticks need to be attached for twenty-four hours for Lyme disease to be transferred. At the end of each day, perform a thorough body check for ticks. If you find one, use a tweezers to remove it. Clean the area with an antiseptic or an alcohol wipe.

The CDC also reports that there are about 30,000 cases of Lyme disease reported each year. Lyme disease is most common in the northeastern United States and the upper Midwest, primarily Wisconsin and east-central Minnesota. Lyme disease symptoms start with a red bulls-eye rash around the bite, fever, headache, fatigue, stiff neck, and muscle or joint pain. If untreated the disease, in some cases, can progress to Bell's palsy (paralysis or weakness on one side of the face), meningitis, chronic joint pain, and heart palpitations. Early treatment with antibiotics has proven successful.

The best protection against all these biters is long pants and long sleeves. In bad swarms, use a head net. For tick prevention the pant legs should be tight-fitting or tucked into your socks. Spray all of your clothing with 0.5 percent permethrin for an extra layer of protection.

If you decide not to wear long clothing, a thorough application of insect repellant that contains at least 30 percent DEET will offer some protection. Insect repellant needs to be reapplied every couple of hours. If you are a wet footer, which you should be, you will have to reapply the repellant to your lower legs at every portage. I find that sunny or windy areas slow mosquito activity. Being on the water also will give you some relief.

Weather

Weather in the Boundary Waters area is unpredictable. You would think that meteorologists can forecast the weather as accurately as anywhere else. The problem arises when you are sitting at home in March planning a July trip. All your planning and preparation cannot foresee the weather. You can always grab a long-range forecast as you leave home, but the accuracy diminishes each day of your trip.

If you plan on spending more than a weekend, there is a good chance the forecast will change. Once you are in the interior of the forest, you'll only get weather updates if you carry a portable radio. A weather radio or an AM/FM will work, but I find reception to be spotty in the northern reaches. I have also found that, even with a weather radio, the weather is not always as predicted. Be sure you have the equipment, shelters, and rain gear to weather the storms.

Thunderstorms, rain, snow

Our biggest trip of the year is usually during the summer solstice. June is the wettest month in the Boundary Waters. We know there will be rain.

On the Frost River in 2007, a storm hit, forcing us to hunker down under some cedars for a couple of hours. Anytime a thunderstorm is threatening, get off the water and find a sheltered area. Lightning can ruin any trip quickly.

In 2009 we traveled the head waters of the Kawishiwi River. Our last night was on Lake Three. Around 2 a.m. a thunderstorm rolled in. We had been watching the leading clouds all day so it was no surprise. As the storm hit, I went out to watch. I sat there amazed as the lightning was nonstop, sending tracers across the sky. Thunder rolled across the lake and shook the ground. The storm lasted about an hour, but by the time it ended, we had two inches of standing water through most of the camp.

In 2012 we were in the Ledge Lake area when it rained for three days. At one point it rained for twenty-six hours nonstop. As we finished our trip and left for home, we found out that massive flooding had occurred in northern Minnesota and were able to see some of the damage as we passed through the Duluth area.

On June 19, 2016, a severe storm passed through the Boundary Waters. As a result, nine people were injured, one fatally. On Duncan Lake, northwest of Bearskin Lake, off the Gunflint Trail, a man was killed by a falling tree. His son was severely injured. West of there, on Clove Lake, along the Granite River, a man was injured by a falling tree. On Sunday Bay off Crooked Lake, north of the Echo Trail, six were injured by a lightning strike. Our corps passed through Crooked Lake four days prior to this tragic storm.

When the temperatures drop, the rain becomes snow. Snow is not unheard of, especially in May or September. During these months do not be surprised if you are knocking ice off your tent in the morning from an overnight storm or morning dew.

Wind

In 1999, a significant meteorological event occurred. A major wind storm, or derecho, hit the Boundary Waters area. This storm started in North Dakota in the early hours of July 4 and ended in Vermont the following morning. Wind speeds were recorded in excess of 100 mph. One person was killed and sixty were injured. It is now referred to as the "Blowdown." Trees were blown over or snapped off in 370,000 acres, or about 32 percent of the Boundary Waters. It damaged 1,500 campsites, 550 portages, and set the stage for wildfires. Other extreme wind storms were recorded in 1988 and 1992.

Wind, to me, is more serious than rain. Open wilderness canoes are not designed to take on big water. When we check the weather forecasts, we usually look for storm fronts. These are important in preparing for rain, but you want to pay attention to the winds. Winds will start to pick up as a front rolls in or out.

You may also experience short bursts of strong winds. In 2008, on the south end of Missing Link Lake, we were treated to a waterspout. It was a mostly clear day. A gust of wind channeled through the creek bottom to the west and created a twenty-foot-tall waterspout. The show lasted about thirty seconds, long enough to enjoy but too short to reach my camera.

In 2011 we gained first-hand experience on Fraser Lake. Winds were ten to fifteen mph and wave heights about one-and-a-half feet, well within the capabilities of our corps. When we were about half way up the lake the winds increased dramatically and the waves doubled in size. One canoe was capsized and a second one swamped. We were able to push to the lee of a bay. Fortunately, there were no injuries and no lost gear. As quickly as the wind picked up, it calmed to what it was when we first entered the lake. This burst lasted about thirty minutes.

During the mop-up of the Pagami Creek Fire in October 2011, a USFS fire crew of three was swamped on Alice Lake requiring rescue by a USFS float plane.

In July 2014, a thunderstorm with strong winds blew down trees in the Lac La Croix area resulting in seven injuries, two requiring evacuation by float plane.

Another concern is the topography. Hills and valleys can channel the winds making them stronger than in other areas. Larger lakes will pile waves up on the downwind side. Islands, peninsulas, and bays can be used to avoid these areas or offer some protection. By watching the wave heights, you can gain an understanding of where the winds are channeling.

Temperatures

As you can see on the chart on page 47, average summer temperatures are quite nice. Problems arise when you look at the extremes. High temperatures rarely get above 84^0 F. With the abundance of drinking water and the coolness of the lakes, heat exhaustion (hyperthermia) really isn't a problem.

Low temperatures may be a problem if you don't plan for them. Many people pack their clothing based on the averages. Low temperatures in July, the warmest month, have been recorded in the thirties. If you plan a trip in May or September, low temperatures regularly go below freezing. If you become wet, whether by rain or accident, the risk of hypothermia increases. Most people are not aware that they are becoming hypothermic. Many summer sleeping bags are inadequate in freezing temperatures.

Signs of hypothermia are:
- Shivering
- Lack of coordination
- Slurred speech
- Confusion
- Drowsiness / low energy
- Lack of concern
- Unconsciousness
- Weak pulse / shallow breathing

Hypothermia prevention starts with the proper clothing. All experts agree with a multi-layering method, starting with warm headgear. If you suspect someone in your group has hypothermia, do the following to rewarm them:
- Get them to a sheltered area out of the wind.
- Remove wet clothing.
- Put them in dry clothing, a blanket, or a sleeping bag.
- Get a fire started, if possible.
- Give warm fluids: water, coffee, tea, soup.

We will cover more about what clothing and gear you will need in Chapter Four and weather threats in Chapter Six.

Sun

Bring sunblock. Sunny days on the water will cook you. Many wilderness enthusiasts preach about using long-sleeved shirts, long pants, and floppy hats. These are all good thoughts. I prefer to enjoy the warmth of the sunshine. That is not to say that I don't take precautions.

Be aware of your exposure to the sun and guard against too much, either by using long clothing or sun block. Remember that sun block washes off. Good sunglasses are a must. Wear a hat to protect your head and a bandanna for your neck. Warm, sunny days on a placid lake are a canoeist's dream.

Boundary Waters Weather

		May	June	July	Aug	Sept
Average	**High °F**	65	73	78	75	64
	Low °F	41	51	56	54	44
Precipitation (inches)		2.87	4.19	3.72	3.84	3.63
Cloud Cover (%)		64	57	45	43	60
Sunrise		5:22	5:06	5:20	5:51	6:24
Sunset		7:58	8:22	8:19	7:45	6:53
Hours of Daylight		14:36	15:16	14:59	13:54	12:29

Records	**High °F**	100 in 1995	
	Low °F	-45 in 1967	
Warmest Month		July	
Wettest Month		June	
Chance of T-storms		July	22 percent
Windiest Month		May	9.5 mph avg.
Calmest Month		July	7 mph avg.

(Data from weatherspark.com)

Wildfires

The title of this section not only describes the area that these fires occur, but also the nature of the fires. I spent thirty-five years as an urban firefighter and have my share of stories to tell, but the work these wildland firefighters do is unparalleled in the fire business. Fires in the Boundary Waters area, or any wilderness area, were, are, and will continue to be a problem. The sheer size (area), access, and the magnitude (intensity) of these fires make it difficult, if not impossible, to control.

The Boundary Waters, the Quetico, and the Superior National Forest are no strangers to large wildfires. Numerous fires were reported in the area by early travelers. In 1875, 192,000 acres burned, and in 1894, 130,000 acres burned.

As mentioned earlier, the "Blowdown" occurred in 1999. The resulting fuel load on the forest floor has made for extreme fire conditions. The area remained relatively quiet until August 2005 when a lightning strike caused a fire between Alpine Lake and Seagull Lake, consuming 1,400 acres.

In 2006, smaller fires occurred near Famine Lake, Turtle Lake, and Red Eye Lake. The largest was a lightning strike fire that started near Cavity Lake in July 2006, which consumed 32,000 acres. In May 2007, a campfire caused the Ham Lake fire, which consumed 76,000 acres in the United States and Canada.

The most notable recent fire in the Boundary Waters and Superior National Forest is the Pagami Creek fire of 2011. The fire started with a lightning strike on August 18. It eventually traveled to the east as far as Polly Lake, consuming 93,000 acres of forest. The smoke was visible from space, and I can personally attest that the smoke smell went as far as Green Bay, Wisconsin, for a number of days.

Fire Suppression

In 1910, a major wildfire in Montana, Idaho, and Washington consuming 3 million acres of forest, provided the impetus for the U.S. Forest Service to increase its fire-suppression capabilities. This period is known as the "Suppression Era." Roads were built, lookout towers set up, communications improved, and ranger stations were established. This policy continued into the 1960s, when foresters found that fire was an integral part of the forest ecosystem. In the early 1970s, the "Let Burn" policy was implemented.

Today the Forest Service utilizes prescribed (controlled) burns to reduce heavy fuel loads in high-hazard areas. They also take an active suppression role if communities or resources are threatened. As communities grow, people, more than ever, are choosing to live in these wildland areas. Since the 1990s, the Forest Service and other fire agencies have taken an active role in educating residents who live in what is called the "Wildland/Urban Interface." Almost half of the Forest Service's budget is spent on fire control.

Before you finalize your plans, check and see where recent fires have been, what the fire danger is, and if there are any active fires. All this information is accessible on the U.S. Forest Service website, by calling one of the Ranger Stations, or by checking with your outfitter.

Fire Prevention

Always use caution when you start a fire in the wilderness. You are surrounded by fuel. Remember big fires start small. More than 80 percent of wildfires are started by human activity, with campfires being the most common cause. When you check the fire danger, you also need to be aware of any fire restrictions and where.

In dry weather, even without restrictions, it is a good idea to forgo a fire and do all of your cooking on a camp stove. When we travel we use the stove to do most of our cooking and only use the campfire for baking and the ambiance. Many times wet weather will prevent you from starting a fire, therefore a camp stove is a must.

A campfire is nice in the wilderness. In some cases, such as with hypothermia, it can be a life saver. The atmosphere that it creates is warm and comforting. But use common sense when you build a fire. The wilderness is not the place for bonfires. Keep it small and manageable. The bigger the fire, the greater the potential for windblown embers.

Your fire needs to be attended at all times. Most nights when we make our camp, we assign a fire tender. Their job is to gather wood, start the fire, stoke the fire, and be sure it is out before bedtime or leaving camp. We rotate this job so everyone becomes proficient at making fires and the responsibility that goes with it. Before we leave, we check the firebox to assure that all embers are cool and to pack out any trash that may have been thrown in.

Fire Survival

Wildfires are not uncommon in the Boundary Waters area and the chances of getting caught in one are slim, but still a possibility. In the Pagami Creek fire, 114 campsites were affected. The fire traveled sixteen miles in one day. Just because you smell smoke, though, doesn't mean you are in immediate danger. The fire may be miles away and traveling in a different direction.

Follow these steps if you encounter a wildfire:
- Most fires follow the prevailing winds, primarily heading east and north. Do not travel into the direction of the fire path.

- Embers may create spot fires downwind of the fire.
- If you find yourself downwind of a wildfire, travel perpendicular to the fire path. Follow larger bodies of water, if possible.
- Keep a close eye on any wind changes.
- Fire activity may decrease in the early morning and late evening due to higher humidity. Travel may be safer at these times.
- Large, tall smoke plumes indicate a very hot fire. If you are downwind, seek a point of refuge such as a large lake.
- If you are trapped by a wildfire, don't panic. The USFS recommends this procedure:

Put on your life jacket and take your canoe into the water. Paddle to the middle of the lake, tip your canoe and go under it. You can breathe the cool trapped air under your canoe until the fire passes.

Leave No Trace Camping

When you are camping, especially in a wilderness area, practice "Leave No Trace" camping principles. The BWCAW Trip Planning Guide lists some practices based on the Leave No Trace Center for Outdoor Ethics principles.

The Leave No Trace Center for Outdoor Ethics is a member organization devoted to teaching responsible camping by raising awareness and educating people about reducing their impact on the environment. Their teaching is based on seven principles.

Plan Ahead and Prepare
- Know the regulations and special concerns for the area you'll visit.
- Prepare for extreme weather, hazards, and emergencies.
- Schedule your trip to avoid times of high use.
- Visit in small groups when possible. Consider splitting larger groups into smaller groups.
- Repackage food to minimize waste.
- Use a map and compass to eliminate the use of marking paint, rock cairns, or flagging.

Travel and Camp on Durable Surfaces
- o Durable surfaces include established trails and campsites, rock, gravel, dry grasses, or snow.
- o Protect riparian areas by camping at least 200 feet from lakes and streams.
- o Good campsites are found, not made. Altering a site is not necessary.
    - o In popular areas:
        - Concentrate use on existing trails and campsites.
        - Walk single file in the middle of the trail, even when wet or muddy.
        - Keep campsites small. Focus activity in areas where vegetation is absent.
    - o In pristine areas:
        - Disperse use to prevent the creation of campsites and trails.
        - Avoid places where impacts are just beginning.

Dispose of Waste Properly
- o Pack it in, pack it out. Inspect your campsite and rest areas for trash or spilled foods. Pack out all trash, leftover food, and litter.
- o Deposit solid human waste in catholes dug six to eight inches deep, at least 200 feet from water, camp and trails. Cover and disguise the cathole when finished.
- o Pack out toilet paper and hygiene products.
- o To wash yourself or dishes, carry water 200 feet away from streams or lakes and use small amounts of biodegradable soap. Scatter strained dishwater.

Leave What You Find
- o Preserve the past: examine but do not touch cultural or historic structures and artifacts.
- o Leave rocks, plants, and other natural objects as you find them.
- o Avoid introducing or transporting non-native species.
- o Do not build structures, furniture, or dig trenches.

Minimize Campfire Impacts
- o Campfires can cause a lasting impact to the backcountry. Use a lightweight stove for cooking and enjoy a candle lantern for light.
- o Where fires are permitted, use established fire rings, fire pans, or mound fires.
- o Keep fires small. Only use sticks from the ground that can be broken by hand.
- o Burn all wood and coals to ash, put out campfires completely, and then scatter the cool ashes.

Respect Wildlife
- o Observe wildlife from a distance. Do not follow or approach.
- o Never feed animals. Feeding wildlife damages their health, alters natural behaviors, and exposes them to predators and other dangers.
- o Protect wildlife and your food by storing rations and trash securely.
- o Control pets at all times, or leave them at home.
- o Avoid wildlife during sensitive times: mating, nesting, raising young, or winter.

Be Considerate of Other Visitors
- o Respect other visitors and protect the quality of their experience.
- o Be courteous. Yield to other users on the trail.
- o Step to the downhill side of the trail when encountering pack stock.
- o Take breaks and camp away from trails and other visitors.
- o Let nature's sounds prevail. Avoid load voices and noises.

For more information and an online training course go to:
Leave No Trace Center for Outdoor Ethics at www.LNT.org

Chapter Three

Planning Your Trip

The first thing you need to determine is what type of adventure you are seeking. Are you looking to explore the wilderness? If exploring is what you desire, it can be as simple as moving between the different lakes or following one of the river systems. You can go see some of the water falls, pictographs, or the geological formations.

Perhaps you want to find a fishing hotspot? If you are a fisherman, you may have heard of a specific lake or lakes to fish or you may want to try your skills on any of the lakes. The bait shops and, especially, the outfitters will be able to give you some guidance.

Perhaps you just want to relax in solitude? Most users of the Boundary Waters travel one day in or use a base camp. Many people will travel four to six hours before setting up camp. And, with the average trip lasting four days, this is usually as far as they go. These are usually relatively easy trips with few portages and you still get a good wilderness experience.

After the first day, if you continue to travel, your contact with other humans drops dramatically. Your experience and trip duration should dictate how far you venture into the wilderness. If you are taking a shorter trip, don't despair. Look for smaller lakes with one or two campsites on them. Or, on a larger lake, look for campsites that are remote. Look for ones that are away from the portages, tucked in the end of a bay, or on the backside of a peninsula or island.

Not all areas of the Boundary Waters are equal when it comes to solitude or wilderness. Ely is the hub for much of the activity around the Boundary Waters. It offers easy access with all of the amenities one would need: lodging, restaurants, shopping, services, and entertainment. It is also close to most of the lakes that allow motorboats. With this to offer these lakes attract most of the visitors to the area. Entry points near Ely and along Fernberg Road are some of the busiest. North and west of Ely, along the Echo Trail, the entry points are less traveled. This entire area has some beautiful pictographs, water falls, and scenery. It also provides access to the Quetico Provincial Park by way of Lac La Croix or Prairie Portage.

As you get farther away from Ely, the areas become more isolated. The south side of the Boundary Waters can be reached from Ely or from Tofte (twenty-four miles by way of the Sawbill Trail), or from Lutsen (by way of the Caribou Trail). These entry points offer many smaller lakes and rivers. It allows for good access to the interior of the Boundary Waters. There are no motorboat lakes. There are few places to purchase supplies, so bring in what you will need. Sawbill Outfitters on Sawbill Lake (Entry Point # 38) can provide for your last-minute needs.

The east side of the Boundary Waters is accessible by way of the Gunflint Trail, extending fifty-seven miles from Grand Marais. The upper end of the trail is nearly surrounded by the Boundary Waters, thereby offering numerous entry points. There are a number of resorts, campgrounds, and outfitters along the trail. Smaller lakes and rivers offer access into the interior of the Boundary Waters. You can also travel along the Laurentian Divide in the Misquah Hills, or venture into the Quetico by way of Cache

Bay on Saganaga Lake. The only motorboat accesses are on parts of Saganaga, Seagull, Clearwater, and East Bearskin lakes.

As with the Sawbill Trail, supplies are limited to the outfitters or resort camp stores. Trail Center, on Poplar Lake, may have the items you forgot. Coffee perhaps?

Appendices 2 and 3 list the daily quotas of the entry points. The more permits allowed, the more people you will see. If you want solitude, choose the less-traveled entry points.

In the Quetico, with the exception of Atikokan, supplies and services are limited. The Quetico is less traveled than the Boundary Waters. Half of its entry points are through the Boundary Waters. When traveling through the Boundary Waters to the Quetico, you will need a Boundary Waters permit, Quetico permit, and a Remote Area Border Crossing permit.

Outfitters

If you plan on going to the Boundary Waters only once or maybe every few years, consider using an outfitter. When you weigh the cost of buying and maintaining your own equipment that you seldom use, it would be cheaper to rent from an outfitter. There are many outfitters who service the Boundary Waters and the Quetico. If you know the area you want to travel in, select an outfitter near there. If you have no preference, any outfitter will be able to help you. See Appendix 4 for a listing.

Outfitters not only provide you with equipment, they are helpful in planning a trip based on your experience, abilities, and desires. They also can purchase permits on your behalf. If you choose the complete outfitting package, they will provide all of your equipment and meals. You need only bring clothing, personal items, and leisure-time items (fish tackle, books, cards, etc.).

You get to choose your meals from their menu beforehand. Breakfasts, lunches, dinners, beverages, and snacks are available, including vegetarian choices. The cost of a full package from an outfitter will run about $150 per person per day, usually requiring a three-day minimum. To some this may seem expensive but if you figure the cost of canoe(s), tent(s), sleeping bag(s), stove, filter, cookware, and meals, it is relatively cheap.

When you arrive at the outfitters, they will orient you to the equipment. They can also coach you in the use of a map and compass and review your planned route. Many can provide you with lodging or camping before you enter the Boundary Waters and after your return.

If you have your own equipment, and only need a few items, these can also be rented from them. Most have a camp store for your last-minute items or souvenirs. Some outfitters also offer, for a fee, shuttle service to and from your entry point, tow service to Cache Bay or Prairie Portage for access to QPP, and, if you still don't feel comfortable, they can provide you with a guide.

Once again outfitters are a great resource for advice when traveling and fishing in the wilderness. A complete listing of their equipment, services, and pricing can be found on their websites.

Trip Options

All trips should start with a plan. If you choose to use an outfitter, much of this can be done for you. Part of the wilderness experience, though, is in planning your own trip. To do this you will need maps. I use National Geographic maps for the rough planning. Fisher Maps and voyageurmaps.com are nice for the details. Appendix 11, Contacts/Resources in the back of the book, has information you will need for purchasing these maps.

Short Trip - This trip is pretty much what I described above. Select a lake, whether for its location, fishing, scenery, or just because. You set up camp and fish, swim, or just relax. You can take short trips to check out lakes and streams. You pack up and head out the way you came in. These trips are generally of a shorter duration, two to four days. This is probably the most common trip taken.

Base-Camp Trip - Base-camp trips are generally longer than the short trips above, lasting five to fourteen days. Base campers will generally push farther into the wilderness to get away from other people. It starts by selecting an area you want to fish or explore. Find a campsite in the middle of this area to establish your base camp. The main benefit of a base camp is you only have to set up and break down your camp a few times, leaving more time for leisure activities. From this base camp you can take extended day trips to fish and explore the surrounding areas. Base camping allows you the ability to travel with minimal gear on your day trips, letting you to move faster and cover larger areas. Remember that you are still in the wilderness and you should always carry your essential gear with you.

Voyageurs Trip - These are the trips I love the most. As Sigurd Olson wrote in his book, *The Lonely Land*, "...we were travelers, and part of the joy to us all were the new campsites each night, new vistas and fishing spots and the great satisfaction of having covered a certain distance on the map." Like the Voyageurs, you break camp every day and push on. This is a much more aggressive trip and requires planning, physical fitness, and knowledge of the wilderness.

These trips last a week or more and generally extend deep into the Boundary Waters and the Quetico. To plan these trips, pick an area you want to travel through. Establish your entry point and plan a route. On some trips, you may be able to loop and return to or near your entry point. Others will require some type of shuttle. Most outfitters can provide this shuttle service for you. Travel distance and difficulty will determine the duration of your trip. If you like river systems, this is the type of trip you will be taking. The bonus to this trip is you will cover a lot of area, see a lot of wildlife, and see few people.

The duration of your trip will narrow down some of your trip options. See Chapter Nine for some trip suggestions.

Travel Time

Part of planning is determining how far you can travel in a given amount of time. This will help you find your first night campsite or help you decide where to place your base camp. If you opted for the Voyageurs trip, it will help you determine the distance you can cover in a given day and the duration of your proposed trip.

Travel time and distance have a number of variables. Let's start with your time on the water. On relatively flat water, a leisurely paddle will get you about three miles per hour. Paddling into the wind or waves will slow you. If you are forced to take a route around the perimeter of a lake due to wind and waves, this will add distance and take longer. If you are fortunate and have the wind at your back, you will travel a little faster -- just be careful of waves piling up on the downwind end of the lake.

On rivers the wind and waves are less of a factor. On the map many of these rivers look straight. In reality many of them meander through the muskegs and vegetation. Some of the shallower rivers have subsurface rock hazards that slow your progress while maneuvering between them. Most portages for rapids are marked on the map but beaver dams are not. Maneuvering your canoe over a beaver dam takes time. Some will have to be portaged.

You would think that on land, portaging would be easier to calculate. In general it is, but be prepared for surprises. You may run across numerous obstacles including deadfall, elevation changes, high water, beaver ponds, wildlife, and other challenges to slow you down.

The amount of gear you pack will also determine how long it will take you to portage. Some wilderness travelers are minimalists and pride themselves on being able to travel and camp with the least amount of equipment. On the other hand, I have seen campers, primarily base campers, who have screen tents, coolers, lawn chairs, and yes, even quarter-barrels of beer. Most travelers fall somewhere in between. They carry enough equipment to get by comfortably, usually two to three packs per canoe. When portaging your pace will average about two miles per hour. The number of trips you take across the portage will determine your actual distance and travel time.

Calculating Travel Time - Start by selecting the route you wish to take or the lake you wish to reach. Total up the number of miles you will be traveling on water. Next, total up the distance in rods that you will be portaging. From this you can estimate your travel time and distance for each day and your entire trip.

On water:
    Lakes - 3 mph
    Rivers - 2 mph
On land:
    Average portage speed is 2 mph.
To convert rods to miles:
    Take the total number of rods and divide by 320 (number of rods in a mile).
    Examples: 371 rods = 1.2 miles
                    585 rods = 1.8 miles

The number of crossings per portage you make will affect your travel time. A single crossing is just that, 100 rods is 100 rods. A double crossing will be three times the distance. And a triple crossing will be five times the distance. Remember not to overload yourself. The double crossing is the most common.

Example 1:
Paddle	6.9 miles divided by 2 mph (rivers)	= 3.5 hrs
Portage	1.2 miles divided by 2 mph (single crossing)	= 0.6 hrs
Total	8.1 miles	4.1 hrs

Example 2:
Paddle	8.3 miles divided by 3 mph (lakes)	= 2.8 hrs
Portage	1.8 miles (dbl. crossing = 5.4 mi./2 mph)	= 2.7 hrs
Total	10.1 miles	5.5 hrs

Example 3:
Paddle	10.5 miles divided by 3 mph (lakes)	= 3.5 hrs
Portage	0.8 miles (triple crossing = 4 mi./2 mph)	= 2.0 hrs
Total	11.3 miles	5.4 hrs

Don't forget to add break time, usually one hour per day.

Boundary Waters Canoe Area Reservations

One of the best ways to get answers to your questions on planning a trip, traveling, or reserving a permit in the Boundary Waters is to visit the U.S. Forest Service website. Go online to www.fs.fed.us. In "Find a Forest or Grassland," select "Superior National Forest." Click the "Go" button. On the left side column of the Superior website, select "Special Places." On the right side column of the Special Places page, select:

- ***BWCAW Trip Planning Guide*** for information on rules, travel, fishing, entry points, and permits. I suggest printing a copy of this guide for reference, or pick one up at a Ranger Station.
- ***What to Know before You Go*** for information on traveling in the Boundary Waters.
- ***BWCAW Rules*** for rules and regulations governing travel in the Boundary Waters.
- ***Entry Point Map*** to help you select the entry point you want to use.

At the bottom of the right side column is the link to www.Recreation.gov. Use this site to reserve your permit.

Permits - So you have planned your trip and have selected a route or destination. Now it's time to get your permit. All entry in the Boundary Waters, even day trips, requires a permit. During your planning you should have determined your trailhead, or entry point. See a map of the entry points and daily quotas in Appendix 2 or online at www.Recreation.gov.

Each permit allows up to nine people and four canoes. Permits are regulated by a quota system and only a set number of groups may enter at each entry point on a given day. The more popular entry points do fill up during peak season. Planning and reserving your permit early is the best way to get the entry point you want. Permits can be reserved on a first-come basis. Some of the most popular entry points (24 and 25) are chosen in a lottery system.

Reservations are accepted beginning the second Wednesday of December. Reservations can be made online or by phone. Each

permit reserved will be charged a $6 nonrefundable reservation fee in addition to the user fees. Overnight user fees are charged per trip; $16 for each adult and $8 for each youth (ages 0-17 years). Permits are broken down by use. The categories are:
- Day use-nonmotor
- Day use-motor
- Overnight paddle
- Overnight motor
- Overnight hiking

Self-Issuing Permits: Permits for day use-nonmotor can be picked up at the Superior National Forest Ranger Station that serves that region or from permit boxes at most of the Entry Points. No daily quota is applied and no fee is charged. Self-issuing permits may also be used by overnight users between October 1 and April 30.

Quota Permits: Permits for all overnight users or day use-motor are required between May 1 and September 30. These permits are good only for the entry point and date specified. These permits can be reserved.

Permits may be picked up the day before or on the date specified on the permit. They can be picked up at the regional ranger station or at the "Issuing Station" you have selected. Most outfitters are capable of issuing you your reserved permit.

If you are new to the area, I would suggest stopping at the regional ranger station to pick up your permit. They have displays and information that will help the first-time visitor. They also have updated information on weather, fire conditions, animal sightings, and are capable of answering any of your questions.

Before being issued your permit, at any of the ranger stations or issuing stations, you are required to view an instructional program on rules, travel, and safety. A short oral quiz follows, so pay attention.

Reserving your Permit - To reserve your permit online follow these directions:

- Log on to www.Recreation.gov.
- If you entered through the Superior National Forest/Special Places web page, you are where you want to be.
- If you typed in the above address, you will need to get to the Boundary Waters page.
- In the "Search" box, type in "Boundary Waters."
- From the drop down list, select "Boundary Waters Canoe Area Wilderness (Reservations)."
- When the "Search Results" page pops up, select "Boundary Waters Canoe Area Wilderness (Reservations)."
- In the "Find Permits" column answer the following:
  o In "Looking For," select the type of permit you want.
  o In "Entrance," select the entry point you wish to use.
    • See entry points by selecting "Permit Area Map" or "Entrance List" from the tabs.
  o In "Dates," enter the date you wish to enter the Boundary Waters.
- Left click the "Search" box.
  o If the "Find next avail. date" box pops up, modify your date or entry point and retry.
  o If "See details" box pops up, left click the box.
  o Verify entry point and date. Left click "Book permit" box.
  o Enter your User name (email) and password.
  o If you are a "new customer," left click on the box and follow prompts to register. Record your password. Hopefully you will use it again.
- On the "Permit Order Details" page:
  o Verify your entry point, permit type, and entry date.
  o Enter "Group Leader" information.
  o Enter "Exit Point."
  o Enter "Exit Date."
  o Enter "Group Size" (nine maximum).
  o Enter "Number Watercraft" (four maximum).
  o Select "Permit Issuing Station." The default will be the regional Ranger Station. You can select one of the "Issuing Stations" from the drop-down list.

- o Enter "Alternate Leader Information." Permits can only be picked up by the Group Leader or a specified Alternate Leader.
- o Read "Know Before You Go" and check the box on the bottom.
- o Left-click "Continue to Shopping Cart."
* Purchase your permit by following the prompts.

National Forest Campsites Reservations

The www.Recreation.gov website can also be used to reserve campsites in all the National Parks, Forests, Campgrounds, etc. Having a campsite close to your entry point the night before your entry date can help you get an early start the next morning. Reserving these campsites is similar to your permit.

Go online to www.Recreation.gov as described above.
* If you typed in the above address, you will need to get to the Superior National Forest page.
* In the "Search" box, type in "Superior."
* From the drop down list, select "Superior National Forest, MN."
* When the "Search Results" page pops up, left-click "Superior National Forest, MN."
* In the "Make a Reservation" column, select a campground.
* On the campground page, enter your data in the "Find Sites" column.
* Make your reservation as described above.

Rustic campgrounds are numerous throughout the forest, but are nonreservable and available on a first-come, first-served basis. If you wish to reserve your permit or campsite by phone, the same information will be asked, so have it ready when you call.

Phone: (877) 444-6777

Quetico Provincial Park Reservations

Quetico is similar to the Boundary Waters in its access and regulations. In the Quetico, there are no designated campsites, no fire grates, and no latrines. You can camp anywhere. There are campsites that are used regularly and they are marked on most maps. If you cook over the fire, you will need to bring your own fire grate. Some campers also bring a portable toilet stool and establish a temporary latrine.

Border Crossing

The QPP is located in a foreign country. When you enter Canada, you need to follow Canadian Customs laws. If your trip enters the park from the Canadian side, you can clear Customs at one of the ports of entry, usually Grand Portage or Fort Francis. To enter Canada, you will need a passport or two other forms of identification. Canadian Customs does operate a seasonal port of entry on Sand Point Lake, north of Crane Lake. This entry can be used if you have a permit for the Lac La Croix region. More information can be found at the Canada Border Services Agency website, www.cbsa.gc.ca.

If you enter the park through Canada and exit to the United States, you will have to report to U.S. Customs at Crane Lake, Ely, Grand Marais, or Grand Portage. You will need proper identification when you report there. Requirements for re-entry by U.S. citizens changed in 2009. Be sure you have the proper documentation. More information can be found at the U.S. Customs and Border Protection website, www.cbp.gov.

If your trip enters Canada through the Boundary Waters, you will need to apply for a Remote Area Border Crossing permit. One permit is good for you, your spouse, and dependent children (younger than 18). It costs $30 and is good for one year from the date of issue. The process could take up to six weeks, so apply early. Apply for your RABC at www.cbsa.gc.ca. Search "RABC" from the home page.

Permits

As in the Boundary Waters, permits are required for entry. In the Quetico there are twenty-one entry points. Quetico also uses a quota system. See a map of the entry points and daily quotas in Appendix 3 or online at the Ontario Parks link below. Permits can be reserved up to five months in advance either online or by phone. Permits are picked up at one of the six ranger stations on your day of entry to the park. Permits for Atikokan, Beaverhouse, or Dawson Trail can be picked up at any of these three ranger stations. Permits for Cache Bay, Lac La Croix, or Prairie Portage must be picked up at that ranger station.

Nonrefundable reservation fees are $11 online and $13 by phone. User fees differ depending on whether you are a Canadian resident, nonresident, and by the area you are traveling in. Quetico user fees are per day, not per trip as it is in the Boundary Waters. Nonresident fees for the northern areas are $15 per day, per adult, $6.50 per day per child (ages 6 to 17 years). Lac La Croix permits are $17 and $6.50 per day. Prairie Portage and Cache Bay permits are $21.50 and $8.50 per day. In addition, there is a $100 deposit.

If you enter the Quetico through the Boundary Waters, you will need a Boundary Waters permit. If you plan on spending the night in the Boundary Waters, you will need an Overnight Paddle permit. If you are heading right to the Ranger Station and into Canada, a Day Use permit will work.

Reserving your Permit

You can reserve your permit online or by phone. To reserve your permit online, follow these directions:

- Log on to www.ontarioparks.com.
- On the Ontario Parks home page, select "Reservations" from the top banner.
- On the Reservations page, select "Reserve online now" from the left side column.
- From the left side "Getting Started" column, fill in the following:
    1. Reservation Type:
        Select "Backcountry" from drop down list.
    2. Arrival Date:
        Enter your arrival date
    3. Park / Campground:
        In the "Park" box, select "Quetico."
        In the "Campground" box, select Back Country."
    4. Site Requirements:
        Enter the size of your group (9 max.)
- In the "Find Sites" box, find an entry point by using the "Map," "List," or "Calendar" tabs.
- Once you've chosen your entry point, select "Details" to get information on picking up your permit.
- When you have completed the above, select "Reserve."
- Review the details, check the "Acknowledge" box, and select "Continue."
- Review the details and select "Start Payment."
- Follow registration and payment prompts.

If you wish to reserve your permit by phone, the same information will be asked of you so have it ready when you call.

Phone 888-ONT-PARK
(888) 668-7275

Itinerary

Now that you've reserved your permits and established a tentative route and destination, prepare an itinerary. Design your itinerary not only as a trip planner, but also as a guide so you can be found. If an emergency would happen at home, if you do not exit when planned or in the event of a natural disaster, it will improve your chances of being located.

Leave a copy of this itinerary with someone at home, your outfitter, or at the district ranger station. Do not depend on your cell phone. Once you leave the urban areas, reception quickly becomes spotty to nonexistent. Once you finish your trip and are out of the wilderness, report to whomever you gave your itinerary to so they know you are safe.

This itinerary should contain:
- Group leader.
- Names of others in the group.
- Entry date, trailhead, and entry point.
- Intended route.
- Alternate routes.
- Anticipated exit dates and exit point.
- Terminal date – the date that the authorities should be notified that you have not returned (usually one to two days after your anticipated exit date).
- You can include your outfitter, ranger station, and/or county sheriff phone numbers.
- In addition, you can add paddle distances, portage distances, elevation changes, or points of interest.

Rich Annen

Chapter Four

Equipment

In this chapter we will look at the equipment you will need when traveling and camping in the Boundary Waters area. There are many options out there from which to choose. I will review a number of them. Frequency of use and cost will help you determine which equipment to purchase. As stated before, if you do not have the equipment, and do not wish to purchase it, you can always rent from an outfitter.

Essentials

The following are the essential items you should have with you at all times. Consider it a survival kit. These items are obviously a part of your camping gear but they also should be with you on day trips. Though rare, there are numerous situations that may strand you overnight. Wind, storms, wildfire, and disorientation are all possibilities. Bring along a separate pack that will hold this equipment for those trips. If you are on the Voyageurs-style trip, this equipment should be easily accessible.

Appropriate Clothing - Anytime you set out, you will want bad-weather clothing. If on a day-trip, pack a heavy shirt, hoody, or coat, long pants, and rain gear for each member of your party. If traveling Voyageur-style, have it easily accessible. Digging through your pack for rain gear or warm clothing while it is raining or cold just adds to your discomfort. All clothing, except rain gear, should be protected from rain and water.

Water - Everyone should start the day with a full container of purified water. Due to the abundance of good water, one container per person is all you need to carry. Bring your purifier along on day trips or have it accessible when traveling. Stopping and refilling along the way is easy whenever more water is needed.

Map and Compass - Anytime you are traveling or away from camp, someone in your party should have a map and compass. When going from lake to lake, it is essential. If you are just cruising on your base camp lake, you may get by without one. But remember -- as the shadows lengthen, things start to look different.

Knife/Multi-tool - When you are in the wilderness, this is one of your most versatile tools. Its uses are numerous. A pocket Swiss Army knife has been a staple for decades. More recently the multi-tool Leatherman has become popular. I also carry a heavy knife in my pack for camp use.

First-Aid Kit - Since I just told you to bring a sharp object, I feel it's appropriate to tell you to also bring a first-aid kit. Seriously, though the above is true, anyone can become ill or injured at any time. You need to be prepared.

Food - Your menu and the food you eat will be discussed in the next chapter. When you are traveling, whether on a day trip or Voyageur style, have snacks and lunch accessible without unpacking. We usually pack cold lunches so we do not have to pull out all the cook gear. Because of your activity you will be burning more calories than you are used to – between 3,000 and 5,000 per day. Having this food available will help you maintain your energy level.

Shelter - Once again I am talking about being away from your base camp. When on a day trip, bring along a tarp. If a storm should hit, or you are forced to spend a night away from base camp, you will have shelter. One of the quickest and easiest shelters is to land your canoes, flip them over, and stretch a tarp over the top, crawl underneath and hang on to the corners. Paddles can be used as poles if needed.

Fire Starter - Most fire-starting kits are small and easy to pack, therefore they should be taken with you at all times. If you are forced to spend the night away from base camp or if someone becomes wet and cold, a fire will provide you with warmth and security. Remember, if forced to spend the night, you will have no sleeping bag to keep you warm.

Canoes

Canoes vary based on use. If you are looking to buy a canoe, make sure it is suitable to your use. Canoes for use in the Boundary Waters area should provide a combination of stability and wave handling as well as good tracking and maneuverability. Outfitters provide some of the best-suited canoes for the Boundary Waters area. You can rent from them or, if you do decide to buy, find out what they are using. You can't beat years of experience. A seventeen-foot tandem canoe is the most popular for use in the Boundary Waters area. The following is a brief review of canoe construction and design.

Materials/Construction - The following are the most common materials used in canoe construction.

Wood - Wood canoes are some of the most beautiful and expensive. You can even build your own. These canoes are usually reserved for the enthusiast. They weigh about seventy-five pounds.

Aluminum - Aluminum canoes have been the mainstay for a long time. They are rugged and will handle abuse better than others. The down side is they are heavy. A seventeen-foot lightweight aluminum canoe will weigh about sixty-five pounds.

Plastic – Molded polyethylene plastic canoes are more suited for the recreational paddler and not to traveling in the Boundary Waters area. They are heavy. A seventeen-foot canoe weighs about eighty pounds. Royalex canoes are lighter and more suited for tripping than molded plastic. A seventeen-foot canoe weighs about sixty-five pounds.

Composites – There are a number of composite canoes made that work well in the Boundary Waters area. They include fiberglass, Kevlar, graphite, and carbon-fiber. Combining these materials and adding additional supports makes for a tougher, more rigid, and lighter boat. Fiberglass canoes weigh about seventy-five pounds. Kevlar canoes weigh about forty-five pounds. Graphite and carbon-fiber canoes weigh about forty-two pounds.

Design - A canoe's speed, stability, and handling are all determined by its design. Canoes are specifically designed for racing, tripping, fishing and leisure, rivers and streams, and whitewater. The basic design starts with the length and width of the canoe. The longer and narrower a canoe is, the faster and straighter it will go through the water, but it will not turn well. Also, because of its narrowness, it can be tippy. A shorter and wider canoe may be more stable and easier to maneuver, but requires more effort to push it through the water.

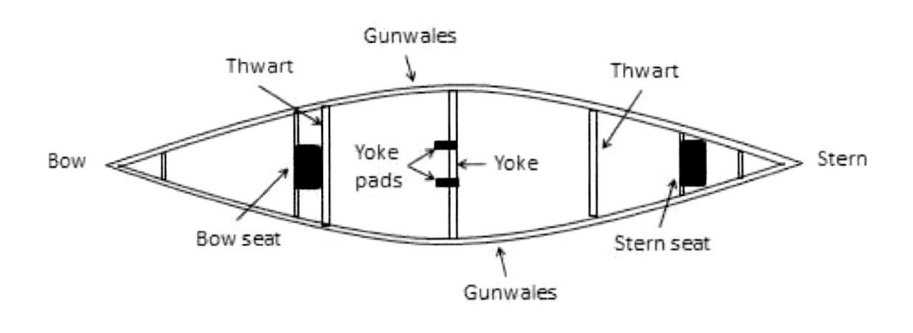

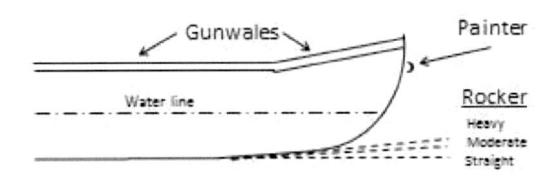

Other design features to be aware of are:

Draft – This is how deep the boat sits in the water. The deeper the draft, the more canoe you are pushing through the water, and the less responsive it will be to turning. It also needs deeper water to travel.

Hull Profile – The hull design is a basic cross section of the canoe. There are four basic hull designs:
   Flat Bottom- Provides the best stability in flat water (initial stability) but becomes tippy in wind, waves, and with body movement (secondary stability).
   Semi-Round Bottom – Provides poor initial stability; handles secondary stability better than the flat bottom.
   Shallow Arch – Is a combination of the above styles. It provides good initial and secondary stability. This design is becoming more popular for beginner and intermediate users.
   Shallow Vee – Similar stability as the Shallow Arch but provides better forward tracking.

Rocker – The rocker is the arch that the canoe has along its bottom from front to back. The flatter the arch is, the better the canoe will track forward, but it will be harder to turn. The more rounded the bottom, the easier it is to turn but will not hold its track as well.

Buying a canoe is like buying a car. There are a lot of options for you to research and to choose. No matter what canoe you decide on, be sure that it comes equipped with a portaging yoke. Portaging yokes are a must for transporting a canoe in the Boundary Waters area.

Paddles

A canoe is not going anywhere without a paddle. The two basic styles of paddles are the straight shaft or the bent shaft. The straight shaft is the one with which we are most familiar. The bent shaft is becoming more popular because it is better suited for seated paddlers. The reason for the bent paddle is that it is more efficient in maximizing the forward stroke.

The tip of the blade, or bottom end, should bend to the front, the cup side of the blade toward the stern. Both styles are constructed of wood or of an aluminum shaft with a plastic or composite blade. You may want to bring an extra paddle in case one gets lost or broken. Tie it to the thwarts until needed.

To select the correct size paddle, place the grip (top) of the paddle between your legs while sitting. When facing straight forward, note where the shoulder of the blade (the point where the blade meets the shaft) lines up. The shoulder on a straight shaft should be at eye level. The shoulder on a bent shaft should be at mouth level.

Solo canoers may want to use a double-bladed, kayak-style paddle. These are paddles that have a blade at each end connected by a shaft. They are usually made of an aluminum shaft with a plastic or composite blade.

Personal Flotation Device

A personal flotation device (PFD) is, by law, something everyone needs. If and when you wear your PFD is your choice. Given there is no one who will rescue you, I recommend wearing one anytime you are on the water. There are many different styles ranging from a seat cushion to the self-inflating vest. The more common types, such as the horse collar or ski jacket, are not well suited for paddling. Ideally you will want one that is designed for a paddler.

Packs

Packs are important in that they are needed to store your gear compactly and securely and provide protection from physical damage and water. They must also allow you to carry them in reasonable comfort over the portages. Packs come in a variety of styles. Some are more suited than others when it comes to canoe tripping.

The number of packs you carry will be dependent on what kind of packs you use and how you configure them. Many trippers carry only one large canoe pack with the camp gear and personal gear packed together. These packs can get quite heavy. Others prefer multiple lighter packs. We generally place three packs to a canoe. Two personal packs and one camp pack. These packs will weigh thirty to forty pounds.

The food bag may be in the camp pack or separate for easy storage later. If separate you may opt for a bear-proof food container. In addition, you may want to bring a small pack to carry essential items you may need throughout the day, negating the need to dig in your main pack. I also carry a small pack with my fishing rod (telescoping) and tackle. The following is a review of some of these packs.

Hiking/Backpacks

Many a backpacker has transitioned from hiking to canoeing. They generally have much of the equipment needed, including a pack. Hiking packs are not the best for canoeing, but they can be used. The problem comes with the frames, external frames being the worst. These frames do not allow the pack to rest on the bottom of the canoe.

Some frames are too long and cannot fit crossways, therefore they must be placed lengthwise and take up valuable space. Some also may have to be angled under one thwart and rest on top of another. When loading a canoe, remember to get the weight as low as possible. Frame side up is your best option with this style pack. By being placed this way, much of your pack may be in water. Hiking packs can be harder to waterproof because of their multiple storage compartments.

Internal frame packs work better but the longer ones will have the same problem as the external-frame packs. Shorter-framed packs, less than thirty inches, may be laid crossways.
To make loading and unloading of these packs easier, limit the gear you hang or attach to the outside of them.

Canoe Style

Canoe packs are obviously the preferred pack for canoe tripping. Their design allows them to conform and sit on the bottom of the canoe. They may be referred to collectively as Duluth packs. The Duluth pack is the perennial pack dating back to the 1880s.

The original is still available along with many other sizes and styles. These packs generally consist of one large compartment. There are numerous manufacturers of canoe packs including Duluth, Knudsen, Granite, Frost River, and Kondos, among others. Their sizes range from 4,000 to 8,000 cubic inches and cost from $150 to $350.

Canoe Pack

Military

Another option for canoe tripping is the military pack. There are a number that work well.

The standard duffle bag with dual shoulder straps is great. Its long, narrow design allows it to lie crossways and under a thwart. The shoulder straps make for an easy carry on portages. We use these for camp gear such as tents, tarps, stoves, fuel, etc. They hold 3,000 cubic inches of gear and cost $10 to $30.

We also use the large ALICE pack. These packs have a short, twenty-inch external frame. It has a large main compartment along with three large and three small outer pockets. When packed they sit upright in the bottom of the canoe, making it easy to load and unload. If need be, two can sit crossways. The frame, hip belt, and adjustable shoulder straps make them ideal for portages. These packs hold 3,800 cubic inches of gear and cost $60 to $80.

Other Options
- ***Pack basket*** – A pack basket is a woven basket that can be inserted into an outer pack or carried by a harness. It is ideal for hauling hard items such as pots, pans, stoves, and fuel cells. They run $70 to $120, depending on the size. A plastic trash container can also be used for the same purpose but doesn't look nearly as cool.
- ***Bear-resistant containers*** - These molded, hard-plastic containers come in different sizes. They range from 700 cubic inches, which will hold about a week's worth of food for one camper, to the 60-liter size that will hold a week's worth of food for a small group. They range from $80 to $160.
- ***Medium ALICE pack*** – A frameless pack with a main compartment and three large outer pockets. Holds 2,400 cubic inches of gear and costs $40 to $60.
- ***MOLLE II duffle bag*** – Works well as a food pack for larger groups or for small groups on an extended trip. Holds 1,000 cubic inches of gear for about $20.

Waterproofing

Your packs will get wet from rain or water in the bottom of the canoe. Do not assume the pack alone will keep your gear dry. Your sleeping bag and clothes are the most important gear to protect. Protect your gear by using a plastic bag that is as big or bigger than the main compartment of your pack. These should be heavy-duty bags. We use 3 mil contractor-type trash bags that can be purchased at most home improvement stores.

Line the pack with the bag. Place your sleeping bag, clothing, and camp shoes/boots in the bag, expel the air, and roll down the open end. These bags can also be used to place your pack in at night to protect it from any rain or dew. You can also use waterproof dry bags. They are available in a variety of sizes. Using both of the above will guarantee dry clothes and sleeping bag. Do not trust

Ziploc bags to protect equipment. You will be disappointed. Also remember that not all your gear needs to be protected from water.

Shelter

I remember when I was a kid we would camp in the backyard using an old military canvas pup tent. Throw an old military poncho down as a ground cover and a couple of old wool military blankets and you were set. For the Boundary Waters area, you will want something more protective and lighter.

Tents

Today's tents are mostly made from nylon with the dome style being the most popular, though many still swear by the classic A-frame. Dome tents are comprised of two or more folding flexible poles that attach at the corners of the tent and cross over in the middle, providing support. Tents vary in size and weight. You will want one that is sturdy enough to survive wind and driving rain. Remember this is your primary shelter when the weather turns bad.

If you buy a tent, be sure the rainfly covers the tent against blowing rain. Shorter rainflies will allow the rain to blow up and in the tent. Zippers leak. The rainfly should protect zippered openings. We add an extra ground tarp to keep ground moisture and dirt off the tent bottom and away from us. If you use a ground tarp, be sure it is smaller than your tent's footprint or run off from the tent will collect between the ground tarp and the tent floor.

When you buy a tent, always figure it sleeps one less than advertised. A two-person tent is actually a solo tent, and a three-person will fit two. A five-person tent (that fits four) is the biggest you will want to use in the Boundary Waters area. The bulk and weight of larger tents make them hard to pack and their set-up size will be tight on many of the tent pads at the campsites.

A three- to five-person tent will range from $80 to $300 and weigh from five to ten pounds. I buy in the moderate range. With proper care, it will last for years. I still have a tent that was our primary tent in the 1980s. Every year treat the zippers to wax or silicone to ease their operation, and every couple of years, apply silicone water repellant to the outside of the tent and the rainfly. I also recommend using the lighter-weight aluminum tent stakes as opposed to the heavier steel stakes or the bulky plastic stakes. As they age, broken or lost poles and stakes can be replaced.

Bivy Sacks, Solo Tents, and Hammocks

If you are a soloist, love the open concept, or just don't like sleeping with other people, you may want to use a bivy sack, solo tent, or hammock. A bivy is basically a cocoon that you place your sleeping bag in. It has a raised area around your head with netting and a rain fly to keep the bugs and rain away. A solo tent is a smaller tent that is just large enough to fit your sleeping bag and a small pack. Both are light, two to three pounds, and cost from $70 to $320.

A hammock is nice in that it gets you off the ground. The drawback is you need trees, which are not available at some sites. Even in the middle of a forest, you may find it hard to locate two sturdy trees the right distance apart. This is especially true if you are traveling in a burnout area. If you do decide to use a hammock, be sure it has netting and a rainfly. It is also a good idea to get one that can be set up on the ground. Hammocks weigh about the same as a bivy and cost from $160 to $350.

Tarp / Screen tent

You will want to bring a tarp along as a rainfly or windbreak. Not every evening is going to be calm and clear. There are different ways to deploy this tarp depending on your situation. We use a twelve-foot-by-twelve-foot green/brown tarp with ten feet of cord attached to each corner and four stakes rolled inside. We also carry fifty feet of quarter-inch cord to suspend the tarp, if needed. Please don't bring a bright-colored tarp. It hurts everyone's eyes.

Heavy-duty poly tarps cost about $10 to $15. I have seen some base campers haul in screen tents or canopies. This is probably nice for extended base-camp trips but I think the bulk and weight is a bit much for your normal trip.

Sleeping bag / pads

Most people who have done any camping will have a summer-weight sleeping bag. Most of these are a cotton blend, weigh four to six pounds, and are quite bulky when stored. Though not the best, they will work but they take up a lot of pack space, are difficult to dry out, and may have to be carried separately.

Ideally you will want a compression-style sleeping bag. They are made of nylon, compress easily, are quick drying, and weigh two to three pounds. For summer camping a 30°F-plus bag will cost between $60 and $200. Remember to always protect your sleeping bag from getting wet.

A sleeping pad is a must unless you like roots and rocks poking you all night. It also keeps the ground chill off of you. The foam/closed cell type are the least expensive at $15 to $35. Thicknesses range from three-eighths inch to one inch. My boney butt needs a little more padding. The other options are the inflatable and self-inflating mattresses. They range in thickness from one inch to four inches, are twenty to twenty-five inches in width, and forty-eight to seventy-five inches long. They range in price from $40 to $230. The thicker, more expensive ones are generally used in cold weather.

Clothing

Below is a listing of some of the clothing options you should consider. What you pack will be dependent on personal preference and the season. While traveling, remember, you will get wet, especially your feet. There have been times I have been thigh deep to load/unload a canoe. I was once waist deep portaging through a beaver pond that cost me a pocket camera.

Layering is the key to staying warm and dry. The level of layering you do will be dependent on the season and the weather forecast. Remember to pack for the extreme temperatures. See Appendix 5 for a clothing checklist.

Innerwear

Go with what you've got. Now is not the time to change what you are comfortable in. During the day you will get wet, therefore I wear my swimsuit underneath. A T-shirt works great, sleeveless, regular, or long-sleeved depending on the temperatures, bugs, or sun. For nightwear in colder weather, good old-fashion cotton or cotton/wool long johns work great.

If you are looking for higher-tech base layering, there are good options available. North Face, Under Armour, Patagonia, among others, make good clothing to meet your needs. Many of the stores have their own brand names; all make base-layer clothing geared to the temperatures you expect to encounter. This clothing is designed to maintain warmth, wick away moisture, and dry quickly. It is made of polyester or a polyester blend.

Outerwear

There are a lot of personal preferences and options out there. The bottom line is you want to stay protected, be comfortable, and be able to work in the clothing you choose. The pants or shorts you wear will probably get wet at some point. Lighter-weight cotton or wool works well. Quick-drying nylon works better. Try to avoid heavier pants such as denim for day travel as they will not dry and have a tendency to bind when sitting in a canoe. Anything that is warm and comfortable is good for nighttime use.

To protect your upper body, there are many long-sleeve options from which to choose: pullovers, button downs, and zippered. These are made from cotton, wool, polyester, fleece, and nylon. For day travel a lighter-weight material works best. Quick-drying materials such as polyester and nylon work better.

Most likely you have something in your closet that will work. If not go online or go to your local sporting goods store to see what's available. At night a heavier cotton or wool shirt will keep the chill away. A sweatshirt or hooded sweatshirt works just as well, but is a bit bulkier. In colder weather, pack an insulated, wind-resistant jacket.

Footwear

Today with the increase in the use of lighter-weight composite canoes, "beaching" a canoe is no longer an option. Wet footing on the portages is now the norm. I see some short trippers and base campers using sixteen-inch rubber boots. I have never tried them.

I have been thigh deep unloading a canoe. They would not have helped. With my luck, I would fill both boots on the first portage.

Some enthusiasts will only wear leather, eight-inch hiking boots. These boots provide good traction and great support. They are ideal for carrying large loads over rough terrain. But these boots become heavy when wet and do not dry out easily. I have also seen travelers using open sandals. I'm sure they are comfortable but they provide no foot protection at all. Don't fret, an old pair of tennis shoes will work fine and are often used.

Comfort, durability, and traction are important. Poor-fitting shoes and, eventually, blisters will turn your trip into a nightmare. Blowing out a shoe mid-trip is not something you want to deal with. Good traction is the most important. You will encounter steep inclines and wet boulders as steep as forty-five degrees. Your shoes better hold or you will be on your ass with a forty- to fifty-pound pack or canoe on top of you. In my experience most injuries occur on the portages.

For most of us, the best option is the water shoe. There are many styles and manufacturers from which to choose. The shoe should drain water quickly. Once you step clear of the water, it should only take a few steps and you should no longer be sloshing in your shoes.

When shopping for a pair of water shoes, use caution when they are labeled "sandals," "watersport," or "boat shoes." Sandals will allow debris in. As a result, you will be portaging with a canoe overhead and a pebble underfoot. Watersport and boat shoes may not provide enough foot protection and most likely they will have inadequate tread. Keen, Teva, Salomon, and others provide good quality shoes. Prices range from $75 to $150.

Once you have set up camp and won't be hiking anywhere, any comfortable, lightweight shoe will work. Tennis shoes, sandals, moccasins, and Crocs are options. I prefer Crocs. They are light, cleanup easily, dry fast, and pack well. In colder weather you may want something warmer. Tennis shoes or a light-weight boot will keep your feet warm. Me, I just wear heavy wool socks under my Crocs.

Rain Gear

Rain is a common occurrence in the Boundary Waters area. For storms that pack heavy rain, wind, or lightning, you will want to hunker down and wait it out. If your intention is to wait out every storm or rainy day, you may be waiting awhile. Rain gear is probably the most underestimated item of clothing. Many travelers believe a simple poncho is adequate. It is not. Ponchos provide no protection for your legs and do not accommodate a pack well.

When traveling in the rain, you will want a hooded rain coat and rain pants. This gear must keep you dry and stand up to the rigors of hauling packs and canoes. Basically, the lighter the material, the less durable it will be. Rain gear also can be used in cooler weather as a windbreaker and will help you maintain body heat. On threatening days keep your rain gear accessible. Columbia, Frog Tog, Carhartt, North Face, and others offer good selections from $50 to $200.

Rain gear is essential.

Camp Gear

Water Purifying

Fortunately, the Boundary Waters area has an abundant supply of clear drinking water. But these waters can carry some of the pathogens that can make you sick. Therefore, you need to guard against them. The most common of these are Giardia (beaver fever) and Cryptosporidium.

Giardia is a parasite that colonizes in the digestive tract of a variety of domestic animals, wild animals, and humans. Giardia may be present in water that has been contaminated by fecal matter. It can be transmitted by poor hygiene, poor dishwashing, cross contamination of cooking vessels, swimming, and, of course, drinking it. Onset is seven to ten days. Symptoms include diarrhea, abdominal cramping, nausea, and gassiness. Most symptoms, in healthy individuals, will resolve on their own in two to four weeks.

Crypto is also a parasite that affects the digestive tract. Its transmission is the same as Giardia. Onset occurs in two to ten days and may last one to two weeks. Symptoms include diarrhea, abdominal cramping, and a low fever. As with Giardia, most symptoms will resolve on their own in healthy individuals.

Viral infections are not a problem in the Boundary Waters area. They are generally reserved for areas with poor water-treatment facilities, such as some third-world countries.

There is much discussion on the transmission of Giardia and Crypto in a wilderness setting. It is now believed that most transmission occurs through poor hygiene. Carry and use hand-sanitizing towelettes, gel (Purell), or soap prior to handling food. Treat all drinking water. Do not contaminate your drinking vessel. All pots used for cooking should have had boiling water in them. This should become a part of your cooking process.

- ***Chemical Treatment*** – You can treat your drinking water with iodine or chlorine tablets or drops. These chemicals will remove bacteria, protozoa, and viruses. Turbid (dirty) water may need higher doses; see instructions on the package. The only bad result is your water now tastes like the chemical used. This can easily be fixed with neutralizers or drink flavoring.

- ***Filtration*** – Filtration is the most common way people purify their water in the wilderness. This is because it is the only way to remove any particulate in turbid water. Filters should be rated to filter to less than 1 micron. Most are in the 0.3 to 0.5 range. This level will remove the bacteria and protozoa including Giardia and Crypto. Chemical treatment is needed to remove viruses.
- ***Ultraviolet (U/V) Light*** – U/V treatment is a newer way of purifying water in the wilderness. It does not introduce any chemicals into the water, it produces no bi-products, and it does not alter the taste. It is effective in killing bacteria, protozoa, and viruses. Turbid water may need a longer treatment time. The biggest drawback is that it is an electronic device that operates on batteries. Electronic devices have been known to fail in wet conditions and batteries have to be replaced.
- ***Boiling*** – One minute, kills everything, done. It's the oldest way to purify water. Drawbacks are it does not get rid of particulates and the water needs to cool.

The best way to prevent any contamination is to filter/treat your drinking water and boil your cooking and wash water. And remember to practice good hygiene. In a pinch, if you are in need of water and away from stoves or purifiers, you can take water from the lake. Find a deeper lake, go to the middle, cover the top of your container and submerge it twelve inches before allowing water to enter. In the early years, this is how we always got our water and we were never sick.

Drinking Water

Carry drinking water with you anytime you are traveling. There are numerous styles and sizes of canteens available. One to two quarts/liters is usually large enough. Remember if you run out, you can stop most anywhere and refill. If you do not have a pocket or space in a pack that is accessible throughout the day, get a canteen that has a carry strap. If you have a pocket that is accessible, then most any container will work. Use canteens, Nalgenes, and even heavier plastic bottles like the ones Gatorade comes in.

Fire Starters

There are three elements to starting a fire in the wilderness. You will need an ignition source, some tinder to ignite, and some fuel. So what do you bring? This is not a survival book, so let's keep it simple.

- ***Ignition source*** – Bring waterproof matches. Put a couple of small boxes in a Ziploc bag. Bring two of these match bags and place them in separate packs. A butane lighter works nice for starting the stove. For an emergency backup, or just to play with, you can bring magnesium, flint/steel, a sparker/igniter, or a compression (piston) igniter.
- ***Tinder*** – This is what you ignite first. Some of the best tinder is in the forest. Duff (dried/decaying brush and grass), pine straw (dried pine needles), birch paper, and dry cedar bark scrapings work best. Or you can use the shredded paper or cardboard from your meal packaging. You can also improve your odds by bringing in store-bought fire sticks. They work well and one is usually enough per fire. Other items you can play with are cotton balls, drier lint, charred cloth, or Fritos.
- ***Fuel*** – Once again some of the best fuel is in the forest. Twigs and dried evergreen branches work great for kindling. As your fire grows, increase it by gradually placing larger pieces of dry wood on it.

To ensure you will always have a fire, bring in some Boy Scout water. You may know it as charcoal lighter fluid. If you do bring Boy Scout water, place it in an eleven- or twenty-ounce fuel cell for protection and to prevent leaking.

The quick and easy way to start a fire that works in most any weather is to build a base of dry tinder and kindling, put a fire stick or two in the middle, sprinkle an ounce or two of Boy Scout water over it, and throw in a lit match. It sounds a lot like cheating but on some wet cold days you won't care.

Wood Cutting

To start and maintain a fire, break or cut some wood. Kindling can be broken by hand. Larger branches can be broken by placing them between two tree trunks that are close together and pushing until the branch snaps. I will caution you not to jump or stomp on a branch to break it. The branch may not be the only thing that snaps. Remember to keep the fire small and within the fire grate. Since you are not building a shelter or cutting down trees, an axe of any size is really not needed.

If you feel the need to split wood, you can use a heavy knife instead, usually one with a thick, six-inch blade. This knife can be used to split small wood by setting the blade on the end of a piece of wood and driving it through using another piece of wood as a hammer. The knife is lighter and more versatile than an axe.

Also bring a folding saw. It is useful to cut bigger branches. More importantly you may need it to clear deadfall from a portage or campsite. The deeper you go in to the wilderness, the less used and maintained the portages and campsites become. It is usually easier to use the saw and clear the deadfall from a portage than it is to break trail with a seventeen-foot canoe. Clearing a trail is also a courtesy to those who follow after you. Many prefer to carry a bigger folding saw but I have found that a seven-inch saw is adequate. But remember there are limitations to this saw when it comes to big deadfall.

Another courtesy to be aware of is leaving wood at a campsite. When you come into a camp, you should find a pile of wood beside the fire grate. This is a tradition that goes back to early travelers. Become a part of the tradition and leave wood for the next camper.

Seating

Once you set up camp, relax. Much of this will encompass sitting down. Sitting on the ground with a tree as a backrest works well, but the tree may not be where you want to sit. Most sites will have logs around the fire grate but offer no backrest or padding. You can always use your personal floatation device for padding.

If these comforts don't suit you, you will have to bring your own along. Your best option is a folding camp seat that acts as a pad and backrest. They are reasonably light and easy to carry. You can even use it in the canoe. There are other lightweight, low-profile folding chairs available, but they can be bulky.

Food Storage

Food storage, by the book, is straight forward. Find two trees, suspend a rope between them, and hang your pack ten feet off the ground. In reality finding two trees, or one tree with a stout branch, is not always easy. Getting a rope over these branches can be a barrel of laughs.

When packing, place your food in a separate bag/pack. This bag/pack can be placed in a larger pack or carried by itself. Or you can buy or rent a bear-proof container. We will review ways of securing your food in Chapter Seven.

Rope / Cord

You will need to bring some type of rope and/or cord to secure your food pack at night. I recommend three-eighths-inch by fifty-foot minimum. I know many will argue that quarter-inch is big enough, but I have seen a lot of quarter-inch cord still hanging in trees after it breaks.

You will still want to bring a length of quarter-inch by fifty-foot cord though, this cord can be used for suspending your rain tarp, as a clothes line, and, possibly, to secure the canoes at night if they cannot be brought out of the water.

When selecting your rope, do not get polypropylene rope. It does not have the strength and it does not hold a knot well. The best is a nylon "braid on strand" (kern mantle) style rope. Its strength-to-weight ratio is good and it can be purchased at most sporting goods or home improvement stores.

Potty Pack

Everyone will need it at some point in time. You can put one together separately or as a group. We put a roll of toilet paper in a one-gallon Ziploc bag, place it in another Ziploc bag (double wrap good; wet toilet paper bad), and add a pack of antibacterial towelettes or gel. In camp this is placed at the trail to the latrine. If the pack is gone, the latrine is in use. Figure about one roll of toilet paper per person per week. You may also want a smaller version in your personal pack just in case you feel the need and the camp potty pack is in the other canoe.

If the need does arise while traveling, use a trowel or stick to dig a hole. Be sure you are away from any water (150 feet is recommended). And please get away from the portage trail. When finished, bury everything.

Lighting

There are many choices here, but remember you want something small and light weight. The best I've seen are headlamps. They leave your hands free and still light your work area. They are also great for reading. In addition, I carry a light that has a focused beam that will project over the lake or into the woods. Smaller Mag-lites and Mini Mag-lites work well.

See Appendix 6 for a camp-gear checklist.

Cookware

Camp Stoves

You will need a camp stove. If you assume you will be cooking over a campfire every night, you will be disappointed. Open-fire cooking is always a treat, but not one to depend on. There are numerous sizes and styles of stoves from which to choose. A one-burner stove is usually adequate. If you are setting up a base camp, have a large group, or are into cooking, a two-burner is an option.

The most-popular stoves will use a canister of propane or propane/butane mix. The propane canisters are sixteen ounces and readily available at most sporting goods stores and some department stores. The propane/butane mix canisters are eight ounces and usually available at select sporting goods stores. The size of the stove and the size of your group will determine the amount of fuel you will need for your trip. For a group of four, you will need about eight ounces per day for a single-burner, propane/butane stove. After a few trips you will be able to fine-tune your fuel needs.

A better option than the disposable fuel canisters is to invest in a stove that uses refillable fuel cells. You have to purchase the fuel cells but they last quite a long time. When you opt for this type of stove, your fuel costs drop considerably. Plus, they have less impact on the environment. Some of these stoves will burn fuel ranging from white gas to vegetable oil. This is usually not an issue, but nice to have as an option. For a group of four, an eleven-ounce cell of white gas will last you two days (twenty ounces, four days). Once again, after a few trips you will be able to fine-tune your fuel needs.

MSR, Optimus, Jetboil, and Coleman, among others, make good, reliable stoves. Costs run from $40 to $150 for a single burner and $50 to $120 for a double burner and are available online or at most of your sporting goods stores.

Pots / Skillet

Your menu selection will determine what you will need for cooking. Unless you decided on all dehydrated meals, you will need a pot or two. The size of the pot(s) depend on the size of your group. There are many self-contained cooking systems available in varying sizes. A one-person combination cook set and mess kit will run about $50. Cook sets with 1.5-liter and 2-liter pots are $50 to $65. The 3-liter and 5-liter pot sets are about $80. A combination cook set and mess kit for four will cost about $100.

You can improvise. Any pot or pots that fit inside each other will do. Leave the glass and cast iron at home. Aluminum, enamel, and stainless pots work well. If it has a long handle, cut it off. Pots with long handles do not pack well or sit well on a camp stove. These pots can be purchased at second-hand stores like Goodwill or St. Vincent de Paul. Pots ranging from 1.5 liters to 2 liters will be less than $10. Remember the lids and don't forget the hot pads. When packing place smaller items inside the pot(s).

Another item you may need is a skillet. Frying food tends to waste fuel so minimize this type of cooking. The one exception is frying fresh fish. This is why we always carry a skillet. Frying fish over an open fire is a treat, but once again don't count on a fire. The skillet can also be used to make desserts. Pan breads and muffins can be baked by using the skillet. If you don't fish or plan on desserts, you probably won't need a skillet. Unlike the pot(s), leave the handle attached.

Also consider a coffee pot. Even if you don't drink coffee, a coffee pot is an easy way to bring water to a boil for dehydrated meals, oatmeal, or hot drinks like cocoa, tea, and, of course, coffee. Some of us prefer fresh-brewed coffee in the morning. My sister, Doris, spoiled us with fresh-brewed coffee and we will never go back to instant.

Cowboy coffee has been the mainstay. Percolated coffee is a treat but also a waste of fuel. Over the last few years, we have started using a coffee (French) press. It's the same as cowboy coffee but without the grit. It's another item to consider, it saves on fuel, and you get your fresh-brewed coffee. As my nephew, Bob, stated, "We can get by without a tent, but not without coffee." Thermos makes a nice 34-ounce stainless/plastic press for about $40.

Utensils

The following is a list of utensils and possible uses. You will not need all of them for your trip. Your menu will determine which ones to take along.

- ***Measuring cup*** – A must for adding measured water to your recipes. It also doubles as a ladle.
- ***Large spoon*** – Needed for stirring and serving meals.
- ***Knife with scabbard*** – Needed for slicing sausages, cheese, or any other bulk food you may bring. I like to keep the food knife separate from any camp or filet knife to prevent contamination.
- ***Spatula*** – Needed if you fry fish or bake desserts.
- ***Pasta spoon*** – Nice for cooking pasta or rice. It also can be used as a serving spoon.
- ***Ladle*** – It is nice for serving soups and stews. The measuring cup will do the same.
- ***Tongs*** – Nice when your menu includes fresh meats or vegetables cooked over or in the campfire.
- ***Cutting board*** – Nice for preparing meats or appetizers. We use a small, square one that fits inside the nine-inch bake pan for packing.

Baking

There are many different ways to bake meals, breads, biscuits, or desserts with a campfire. The question is whether or not you want to bring the extra equipment and supplies. Not all methods of baking are practical in a wilderness setting. Many of the recipes you come across may require a Dutch oven, baking pits, or bulky spits. These are impractical or illegal in the Boundary Waters.

Fires must remain inside the fire grate. But if you do have a good fire with good hot embers, almost anything can be baked. We have baked potatoes, corn, fish, and foil packs containing potatoes and/or vegetables, and/or beef, ham, or sausage. For the foil-pack meals, we use an indirect heating method. The only equipment needed for these foil packs are heavy-duty foil and a little oil or water. The drawback is the packing in and out of any foil used.

Most of our baking is reserved for desserts. Over the years we have had many successes and almost as many failures. A nice, toasty dessert is always a treat, even if it might be slightly burned as sometimes happens. It is also a form of entertainment as the evening winds down.

- ***Reflector Oven*** - There are a number of methods used to bake desserts. The easiest method is to use a reflector oven. It is relatively light and fold up for easy packing. Combine this with a nine-inch baking pan and you will have dozens of options for desserts. The drawback is they are costly, usually running around $80. If you are handy, you can build your own.
- ***Skillet*** - A simpler method is to use your skillet. Pan bread, corn bread, and slab muffins all can be baked in your skillet. See Chapter Five.
- ***Pie Iron*** - Another option is to bring a hand-held, square pie iron. These are usually about two to two-and-a-half feet long. With a little ingenuity you can remove the wood handles, cut down the shafts, and replace the handles so the iron is only about 18 inches long. It makes for better packing. These irons are great for making individual baked breakfasts, lunches, and dinners. You can make traditional pudgy pies (bread and pie filling) and, with practice, it can be used to bake cookies or flat muffins. They cost about $20 apiece.

Mess Kit

Your mess kit is what you use to eat. There are many options available. You can purchase a cookware set that comes with mess kits nestled inside. You can use an old military surplus kit. The Boy Scouts use a kit that holds a cup inside a small pot locked by an arm between a small skillet and deep plate. Bottom line is any metal or durable plastic deep dish will work as a plate or a bowl. Even a metal pie tin can be used.

You will also need a cup for drinking. There are a number of options. Enamel cups are nice but some tend to conduct the heat of the beverage and can be hot to hold. Plastic or stainless-steel travel mugs work great. Plastic camp cups are lightweight, durable, and inexpensive. Ceramic mugs don't work so well.

Your eating utensils should include a fork and spoon. Knives usually are not needed for most recipes. A combination fork, spoon, and knife (Spork) works well and is cheap ($3). You can also get utensils that fold or swing out for use and then pack up neatly. The utensils should fit inside you mess kit. If you do not have an enclosed mess kit, place your plate/bowl, cup, and utensils in a Ziploc bag.

Cleanup

Once all the eating is done, you need to clean up. Bring a combination scrub/sponge pad and a small container (four ounces) of dish soap. You can use the biodegradable type if you prefer. You will find that you will use very little dish soap. Place both the soap and pad in a Ziploc to prevent leakage in your pack. You can throw in a dish towel if you like or the dishes can air dry.

See Appendix 7 for a cook-gear checklist.

Miscellaneous

Navigation - You must have some way of navigating or you will get lost. I prefer a map and compass. Be sure you have all of the maps to cover your entire trip. It is also a good idea to place your map in a large Ziploc bag, a clear dry bag, or a map case. This will keep your map dry and allow you to access it easily. If you are a techno junky, you can bring a GPS receiver. Just remember it will be wet outside.

Fishing gear - There are a lot of options and personal preferences. Talk to any fisherman and you will get different opinions regarding what tackle to bring. Most outfitters can give you some direction. Just remember to keep it compact. A telescoping or two-piece rod makes for an easier carry on portages. One option is to lash the rod to the thwarts of the canoe. Tackle boxes should also be compact. Bring only the minimum of what you truly need. See Chapter Eight and Appendix 10.

Radio(s) / Phones - There are three different types of radios you may want to consider. For longer trips a weather radio is nice to keep you aware of changing weather conditions. It is probably not necessary to bring one on short-duration trips. A forecast the day before your trip starts is usually good enough.

An AM/FM radio can get you weather reports also but reception of the local stations is spotty and you may have to listen for a while to get a weather report. Most of these reports are not as complete as the weather radio. In the northern reaches, the Canadian stations report the temperatures in Celsius. For the non-Canadian/Europeans, it's always a fun time converting Celsius to Fahrenheit while sitting around the fire.

Portable two-way radios are nice if you are in a larger group. We have used them when we split up. We can follow different routes and remain in contact, if need be. When on larger lakes we split up to search for a campsite. For most of our trips we use the radios sparingly.

I have found that cellular phone reception is spotty or nonexistent around the perimeter of the Boundary Waters area. I can't say what the reception is like in the interior of the area since I have never taken one in with me; it stays in the truck. If you truly cannot sever yourself from that other world, you can rent a satellite phone. They run about $20 per day and $2 per minute.

Toiletries - Keep it simple and light. A tooth brush, tooth paste, comb, lip balm, and items like contacts, contact solution, sun block, aloe/lidocaine lotion, and personal-hygiene items are all you will need. You may have noticed that I did not list soap. We have found that for most trips it is not needed. A quick dip in the lake is usually sufficient. Besides, all soaps pollute the water.

Camera - A camera is a great way to catch a lot of memories. A small pocket camera is usually sufficient for documenting your trip. If you are into photography, you will want a better camera. You will be treated to some nice photo opportunities. We have even shot video of wildlife or special camp activities. Look out Les Stroud. Remember to keep your camera(s) protected. You will find yourself in a very damp environment. I have lost two cameras thus far to rain and water.

Repair Kit - Consider bringing a repair kit for longer trips. This kit can include vinyl patches for mattress repair, self-adhesive nylon patch for tent or pack repair, thread and needles for torn clothing or emergency sutures, a small tube of Super Glue, and most important, duct tape. For short trips a small roll of duct tape may be all you will need. Not only will it do all of the above, it can also be used for emergency canoe repair, blister prevention, and as support for a sprain or strain.

Other
- ***Permit/identification*** – Do not forget to bring your Boundary Waters permit. Get caught without one and it quickly ends your trip. It's also a good idea to bring some ID, though you probably won't need it. I joke with my brother, Rod, saying it's to identify his body if they ever find it.
- ***Cash/credit card*** – Sounds foolish, but if you have to bail out mid-trip, it may help you get to town or back to your vehicle.
- ***Medication*** - Be sure to bring any medications you will need and let your travel partners know of your condition(s).
- ***Insect repellant*** – You'll need it. Bring 30 percent DEET or better.

- ***Carabiners*** – A couple small carabiners may come in handy.
- ***Book*** – If all goes well you should find that you have some down time to relax. I enjoy reading. Take a book along; might I suggest this one.
- ***Compact binoculars*** - They are great for watching wildlife. They are also useful when entering a lake in windy conditions to see the wave heights and to chart sheltered areas. We also use them to see if campsites are occupied. It might save you a trip across the lake.
- ***Glasses case*** - If you don't wear your glasses all the time, it will keep them safe.
- ***Notepad*** – Start a journal of your trip. Note memorable portages, lakes, geography, and events.
- ***Ziploc bags*** – Bring a couple gallon-sized to place leftovers in so they don't leak in your food pack.
- ***Hot pads*** – They will make handling hot pots easier.

See Appendix 8 for a personal-gear checklist.

I have listed a lot of different equipment to consider. Remember you want to bring only the items you are going to need. The type of trip you take, the duration or your trip, the weather, meals, and what activities you wish to enjoy will all have an impact on what equipment you take along.

Chapter Five

Meals

Planning your meals is just that, planning. You want to carry enough food to sustain yourself and your group for the duration of your trip. You do not want to go hungry. On the flip side, you do not want to carry more food than you will need. Everyone's appetite is different. Consider that you may be burning more calories per day than you are used to and your appetite will increase. For example, a single-serving size for many meals is one cup; this is not enough for me after an active day. There are numerous options for meals. They may be as simple as prepackaged, freeze-dried/dehydrated meals, or you may opt for your own personally designed dishes.

Part of your meal planning is in the packaging. Glass and metal containers are not allowed in the Boundary Waters or the Quetico. The exception is fuel, repellant, reusable containers, and personal items that cannot be repackaged. Any plastic containers you use, including bags, must be packed out by you. Some of your meals may need to be repackaged. Many store-bought packages are bulkier than necessary and may not be waterproof. Re-sealable plastic bags (Ziploc) work well and come in a variety of sizes. I recommend using freezer bags. They are thicker and more durable.

The type of trip you plan on taking will affect your meal selection. If you are planning a short-duration, short-distance trip or are going to be base camping, you may choose to bring a small cooler. This gives you the option of using more fresh/frozen foods. If you do decide to bring in fresh food, especially meats, you need to plan your packing more carefully. If in doubt bring only nonperishable meals. If you are planning a voyageur-style trip, your fresh food will be limited to the first couple days.

Food preparation is also a factor. If you are base camping, you may have more time for cooking and cleaning. If you are traveling every day, you will want to keep meal preparation and clean up quick and easy with limited fuel use.

Meal Options

Subsistence hunting and fishing - In the old days, this is how wilderness camping was done. Those days have passed. Hunting is out of season for most of the prime camping season. Fishing is in season and many still take advantage of the opportunity to catch fresh fish. Just don't plan on it.

I have yet to meet a fisherman who can guarantee fresh fish on any lake on any given day. That is not to say that if you fish you may be rewarded with a delicious fish dinner, just don't count on it as one of your meals. Even if you catch fish it may not be enough to feed everyone. Use it as a substitute for all or part of one of your planned meals.

Freeze-dried/dehydrated meals - This is the quick and easy way to provide meals for your wilderness trip. Each member of your party can choose their own meals. But it comes at a price. Meals are available from breakfast through dessert. There is a wide variety and most sporting goods stores carry them.

The stores geared to camping will have a larger selection. Mountain House (mountainhouse.com) and Backpackers Pantry (backpackerspantry.com) are two of the bigger suppliers. If you

Don't count on fishing to meet all of your meal needs.

go to the supplier's website, you can see their entire selection, including gluten-free and vegan selections. Don't forget about military MREs (Meal Ready to Eat). Go to your local army surplus store or query MREs to get a list of online suppliers.

For a homier feel to your meals, stop at Trail Center on the Gunflint. They make their own dehydrated meal packs under the Camp Chow name. They have a wide selection and you can talk directly to the chef. You can also check out their selection or order online at trailcenterlodge.com.

Store-bought - There are a variety of meals and products that will work in your wilderness menu available at your local grocery store. Generally, the larger the store the bigger the selection. Shop around and see who has the best selection. Be sure and read the instructions to determine if it is practical to prepare in the wilderness.

Ready to eat - Due to our hurry-up society, there is a pretty big selection of quick meals designed for microwaves. These meals come in a microwaveable package; this means no metal or glass. Hormel offers a variety of beef, chicken, and turkey dishes over potatoes, dumplings, and noodles. Barilla offers pasta options. And Dinty Moore is still putting out beef stew. Most come in a single-serving size. Once again check the serving size to see if it is adequate. No need for a microwave; the meal can be removed from its packaging and warmed in a pot over the stove or campfire. The downside is the amount of plastic packaging for a limited quantity.

Box dinners - Other packaged meals such as Hamburger Helper, Chicken Helper, or Tuna Helper come in a wide variety of flavors. Ground beef can be substituted with dried beef or cut up sausage. Chicken and tuna are readily available in soft packaging. All can be jazzed up with any vegetable of your choosing.

Rice - You will have a large variety of rice and flavorings from which to choose. It is a one-pot meal that you can add a variety of meats and vegetables. My favorite is Zatarain's, but Uncle Ben's, Rice-a-Roni, and many store brands will work. Read the package and be sure it does not require pan frying.

Pastas - Pastas are another great choice. They pack easily and come in a variety of styles. Spaghetti, linguini, and egg noodles are the ones we use the most. They can be topped with many sauces, meats and gravies. Ramen Noodles can be used for a quick hot lunch or as a backup meal. We each carry at least one in our personal pack in case the food pack gets lost, trashed, or stolen.

Potatoes - Instant mashed potatoes are quick and easy. You can add many different gravies, meats, or vegetables. They come in single-serving packs or in bulk boxes. If you buy in bulk, you will have to repack to plastic bags as the cardboard boxes they come in are not waterproof.

Soups - Knorr, Lipton, and many store brands offer soup packets; just add water. They come in a wide variety including beef, chicken noodle, split pea, vegetable, and potato. Once again a variety of meats and vegetables can be added to make a heartier meal. For thicker soups, use less water. For quick hot lunches, don't forget Lipton Cup-o-Soup.

Vegetables – Libby makes precooked, vacuum-sealed vegetable packs that require no refrigeration. You can choose from corn, peas, beans, carrots, and mixed vegetables. Though a little bulkier, they are cheaper and easier to prepare than dehydrated vegetables.

Gravies - There are a variety of gravies that can be used in recipes. Each packet generally makes one cup of gravy. Pick your flavor and add water.

Sauces - Sauces are a little harder. They may require other ingredients like tomato paste or butter. Tomato paste can be made from tomato powder or repackaged from cans. Another option is to find tomato/marinara sauce in a soft pack (Pomi, Hunt's). It's bulkier so eat it early in your trip. Alfredo sauce is also good but it takes longer to cook and requires constant stirring to keep from burning.

Meats - Meats can be added to any number of recipes. To find ones suitable for packing in to the wilderness, go to the Canned Meat aisle of your grocery store. Remember no glass or metal is allowed so find ones that are in soft packaging, including tuna (Sunkist, 2.6 and 6.4 oz.), chicken (Tyson, 7 oz.), ham (Spam slice, 2.5 oz.), or dried beef (Armour, 4.5 oz.). With these meats, once you break the seal of the packaging, they should be used. They do not keep well without refrigeration. Sausage is another option. Summer sausage seems to be the most popular but look for others to add different flair to your recipes or as an appetizer. Sausage keeps better than the other meats and will generally be good for a number of days after opening.

Fruits, nuts, beans - These are a good, lightweight addition to many of your meals. Dried fruits and/or nuts can be added to oatmeal, cereal, and trail mix. Beans are a good protein source that can be added to your dishes instead of meats. Hummus makes for a great appetizer dip.

Fresh/frozen - Fresh or frozen food can be taken along but requires extra care. We limit our fresh vegetables to corn on the cob and potatoes because they can be cooked in or on the campfire. You can bring fresh meats, too. We have had brats, chicken breasts, and pork chops grilled over the campfire. It is usually best to cook these on your first night.

Another option is to precook and freeze some of your meats. We have done this with beef tips, diced chicken, and spaghetti, burrito, or fajita meats. Raw meats take too long to cook on a camp stove and, therefore, use up too much fuel. Precooked meats only need to be warmed. The problem with bringing these meats is leakage and spoilage. To prevent leakage, freeze the meat in a plastic bag, wrap the bag in newspaper, and place it in another plastic bag and refreeze it. Keep frozen until the start of your trip unless you plan on eating it the first night.

Preventing spoilage is not as easy. The best we have found is to keep the frozen meat protected deep in the food pack or in a cooler. If you are traveling every day, the bulkiness of the hard-side cooler makes for a tougher portage. There are many small soft-sided coolers that will work better. A frozen meat pack will take one day to thaw, two days if it is in a cooler, and three days if you pack it in dry ice. You may be able to stretch this an additional day in cooler weather. Keep this pack/cooler out of the sun as much as possible. In the morning remove your evening meal from the cooler and allow it to thaw in the food pack throughout the day. Once the cooler is empty, it makes for a great trash container.

Outfitter-supplied - An outfitter can provide you with meals that have stood the test of time. These businesses have provided thousands of meals to wilderness canoeists. Most have a varied menu from which to choose. Outfitters are listed in Appendix 4 and most of their menus are viewable online. These menus can also give you ideas for planning your own meals.

Meal Planning

Now that you have an idea of the meal options available to you, you need to make some choices. Each type of meal needs to be determined for your entire group. It makes no sense if one person is eating a cold breakfast so you can get an early start, while the next one is having eggs and pancakes. So each day determine what type of breakfast, lunch, and supper your group will have.

Do you want everyone in your party responsible for their own meals or do you want to have all your meals prepared and eaten as a group? How elaborate do you want your meals to be? Remember the more elaborate the meal, the longer the preparation (fuel) and cleanup.

You may want to use a combination of the above. When we travel each member is responsible for their breakfast, lunch, and snacks. Our breakfast preparation consists of coffee and a large pot of hot water. Our lunches are cold. For suppers we prepare and eat as a group. These are planned meals with different members helping each night.

On a recent trip, we spent $250 on food for a party of four. This included breakfast, lunch, snacks, appetizers, supper, and dessert. On our five-day trip that comes out to $12.50 per person per day.

This meal plan works for us because we move every day. Hot water and coffee are ready by 8 a.m. We try to set up camp by 3 or 4 p.m. This allows us leisure time for fishing, exploring, or just relaxing. It also allows time for meal preparation and cleanup.

Breakfast - There are a number of options for your breakfast. You may choose a cold breakfast. Breakfast bars, fruit bars, or Pop Tarts are quick and easy. Cereal in a plastic bag with dried milk is another option. Just add water and shake it up.

If you wish for an easy hot breakfast, a pot of hot water is generally all that is needed for instant oatmeal and freeze-dried meals. Add dried fruits or nuts for a little extra treat.

If you desire a bigger breakfast, you can make eggs, eggs and bacon, or eggs and sausage from freeze-dried packets. You can also make scrambled eggs (use Egg Beaters or similarly packaged eggs) and pancakes (Bisquick, Aunt Jemima). For syrup, buy a small plastic bottle or go to your local fast-food joint that serves breakfast and get some individual serving packs. These large breakfasts require more fuel and greater cleanup. If you are traveling light, this is not the best option.

Lunch - Cold lunches are as simple as trail mix, granola bars, fruit bars, string cheese, or beef jerky/meat sticks. You can also make sandwiches by using thin buns. Look for Brownberry's Sandwich Thins, Country Hearth's Slender Rounds, or something similar. These breads pack better than regular loaves of bread. You can also use pita pockets or tortillas. Add tuna salad, chicken salad, peanut butter and jelly, or a Spam slice. Go to your local fast-food joint and get packets of mayonnaise, mustard, or ketchup to add to your sandwich.

Hot lunches are a good option to have available if you get laid up by the weather. They usually only require heating up some hot water. Lipton Cup-O-Soup or Ramen noodles are quick and easy. Dehydrated beef stew, chili, and assorted soups are also available. A warm meal will always cheer you up on a cold or rainy day.

Supper - If you choose dehydrated or ready-to-eat meals, your options are pretty straight forward. Select the meals you want and you are set. Box dinners are generally more than one serving, so you will have to find a partner or two.

You may choose to prepare your own recipes. Coming up with your own dish is easier than you think. Determine the base for your meal: rice, pasta, potato, soup/stew. Next decide what you want to add: chicken, beef, ham, tuna. Maybe even a vegetable: corn, peas, beans, carrots. Finally, what type of gravy or sauce, if any, you wish to add: chicken, home-style, brown, tomato, marinara, or Alfredo. Now determine what your serving size is and multiply it by the number in your party.

Which type of meal you use may vary with the length of your trip. For the first few days you may use fresh or frozen foods, towards the middle more of the packaged meals, and near the end add in some dehydrated meals.

Snacks - Snacks are always good when you are traveling. You may be more active than usual and your caloric needs will increase. It's nice to have a little something to nibble on. Some choices are trail mix, granola/fruit/energy bars, sunflower seeds, or candy bars.

Beverages - You may or may not want to bring flavoring for your drinking water. The taste of the lake water, for the most part, is good. There may be some lakes that have a hint of iron or tannin to them. Or you may want to bring some flavoring along just to add variety. You will drink two to three liters of water each day. Country Time, Crystal Lite, Kool-Aid, Mio, and many others offer a wide variety of flavors. Individual packets work best. Get the ones that are complete and you only need to add them to the water.

Warm drinks are important if you are traveling in the early or late season. The nights do get chilly and a warm drink is welcome to start or end your day. Coffee is the odds-on favorite. Cocoa and tea are also easy to pack and prepare. Some have also been known to end the evening with a little sip of bourbon.

Appetizers - Appetizers are, for the most part, a luxury. Most of you will have no use or space for them. We eat our lunches on the go most of the time and, when we hit camp, it is nice to have a little something to munch on, enough to tide us over until supper is ready. Some that we have tried include sausage and cheese, pita pieces and humus, or cocktail rye and a vegetable dip. When you are packing and find you are running out of room, this is what gets kicked out. If not, enjoy.

Desserts - Here is another one of those luxuries. We started doing desserts more as a challenge. The challenge was to bake corn bread or a pan muffin by campfire without burning it. It also adds some entertainment to the evening. Go to the Baking Aisle and read the packaging. Most bread or muffin mixes that don't require eggs will work. Don't forget pudding. Puddings are easy to pack and prepare. There are also a variety of dehydrated desserts available.

Baked Goods - You can add to any entrée by serving bannock (pan bread) or baked biscuits with it. It will require additional equipment and time, but can be well worth it.

Miscellaneous - Some of the meals you choose to bring may require more than just water. Below are some items that can be used:

Milk – Dried milk works great in any recipe calling for milk. Measure the amount and place in an appropriate-sized plastic bag. When needed, add water and mix it until the powder is dissolved.

Butter/Oil – Some of your meals will call for butter. A frozen stick will last a few days if protected, or you can use vegetable oil. I use only half the recipe amount when substituting oil for butter. Total up the amount of oil you will need for all your meals and add extra for fried fish. Vegetable oil comes in smaller plastic bottles that work well. Pack the bottle in a protected area or place it in a plastic bag to prevent leakage.

Seasoning – The pre-mixed recipe packets work best but you can pack your own. Measure the amount called for in the recipe and place it in a plastic bag. Place the bag with the rest of the recipe ingredients. If you are a salt and pepper person, you can buy picnic-sized shakers or grab some packets at your local fast-food joint.

Tomato sauce – Tomato sauce can be made from tomato powder. You can also repackage canned tomato sauce to a plastic bag; just use it during the first couple days. For either of them just place the recipe amount in a plastic bag. When the time comes, add water and seasoning to the bag and mix it up. You now have a bag of spaghetti or marinara sauce. Be sure the bag is large enough to hold all the ingredients.

Cheeses – Cheeses are a good option that can be used as toppings on some dishes, as a quick lunch, or as an appetizer. Keep them sealed in a plastic bag and protected in a pack. Cheese, especially block, can last for days.

Coffee creamer – If you like cream in your coffee, as I do, you will be happy to know that Coffee-mate comes in small containers. You can also get the little single-serve packets or you can use dry milk.

Eggs – Here is one thing I avoid. Not the dehydrated breakfast eggs, which are a mixture, but raw or powdered eggs for recipes. Raw eggs are too fragile, the packaged eggs (Egg Beaters, etc.) do not keep well, and powdered eggs are too expensive. If you find a recipe that requires eggs, keep looking. There are other options from which to choose.

Serving sizes - Some suggested serving sizes, per person/day or meal.

    Oatmeal: Two packets of instant oatmeal or one packet if adding fruits or nuts.
    Fruits or nuts: ½ cup.
    Cereal: Place 1½ cup of cereal with 2/3 cup dry milk in a plastic bag. When it's time to eat, add 1 cup of water and swoosh it around. You can eat it right out of the bag.
    Trail mix: 1 cup.
    Beef jerky/sticks: Two.
    Soup: 1½ to 2 cups, depending on additions.
    Rice: 1½ cups for meals; ¾ cup if served as a side dish.
    Pasta: 3 to 4 ounces.
    Mashed potatoes: 1½ cups. 1 cup dry mix makes 1½ cups mashed potato.
    Tortillas: Two 8-10 inch.
    Meats: 4 to 5 ounces for supper meals, 2 to 3 ounces for lunches. This includes chicken, beef, dried beef, ham, tuna, or sausage
    Vegetables: ½ cup.
    Beans: ½ cup.
    Gravy: ½ cup.
    Sauce: 1 cup.
    Mushrooms: 2 ounces.
    Cheese Topping: ¼ cup, prepackaged (Parmesan) or fresh/frozen.
    Beverage flavoring: Enough to flavor two to three liters.
    Coffee: 2 cups.
    Tea: Two tea bags.
    Oil: 1 tbsp. of oil = 2 tbsp. of butter.

Repackaging/Packing

Now that you have established your meal plan, you will want to repackage some of the items. The best way to protect your food against bears is to be sure it is packaged properly and odor free. Many meals come with a foil or plastic pouch inside a box. Get rid of any outside packaging if you can. It is usually bulkier than necessary. If you need the cooking directions, cut it out and put it with the repackaged food. You don't want to bring an entire box if you are only using half of it. Additionally, some of your ingredients may not be in water/leak-proof packages.

If you are using your own recipes, it is easier if you package each meal separately. Calculate the quantity of each dry ingredient you will need based on serving size and the number of campers in your party. If you can utilize the sealed store packaging, do so. If not place the ingredient in an appropriate-sized plastic bag. Place all of the individual ingredients (pasta, meat, gravy mix, etc.) for each meal in a larger plastic bag and seal it. When it is time to prepare this meal, you only have to pull out one bag from the food pack. The exception is the fresh/frozen foods that should be stored separately. Use the plastic bags for mixing ingredients and trash storage.

Now that you have repackaged your meals, you need to put some order to them. Determine the approximate volume of all your food. You need to know this so your food pack/container is large enough to fit all the food. For smaller groups, this can be a smaller pack/container placed inside a large camp pack. For larger groups or longer trips, you will want a separate pack/container.

If members are responsible for all or part of their own meals, have them place their meals in an individual food bag. After breakfast each member grabs their beverage mix, snacks, and lunch for the day. The rest is placed back in their individual food packs then stowed in the group food pack. It is easier for portaging and securing your food at night if all the food is in one pack/container.

When packing, place your meals in reverse order so your next meal is easily accessible. For larger groups, place the suppers toward the bottom and the individual breakfast/lunch packs towards the top for easy daily access.

If you are using a hard-side, bear-proof container, once you secure the lid you are in good shape. If you are using a soft pack, you may want to add a little more protection. We line our food pack with a large plastic bag. Squeeze out the excess air and roll down or zip the top of the plastic bag securely. Secure the pack with its closure. If you choose to bring a cooler, it can be placed in the food pack/container or carried separately.

Appendix 9 includes a list of some of the meals we have used over the years.

Cooking

Now that you have established your meal plan, here are a few cooking tips.

Grilling over a campfire - It is best to cook over hot embers rather than an open flame. Establish a fire that has a good bed of hot embers. You may want to bring in your own grate to place over the top of the USFS grate. Heavy-duty aluminum foil will also work. Fresh fish, hamburgers, brats, chicken breasts, pork chops, and steaks are some options. Bring in only boneless meats and you won't have to worry about packing out bones.

Cooking fresh meats over the fire does present a number of problems. First, you have to deal with the meat itself, keeping it fresh and preventing leakage in your pack. Second, the drippings will contaminate your campfire and attract unwanted visitors. Third, if you brought in your own grate, you will be carrying it around the rest of your trip.

Fresh fish can be seasoned or breaded and fried in an oiled skillet. Fish can also be poached in a foil pack. Seal the fish loosely in the foil with seasoning and some water. Place over hot embers. It only takes a few minutes per side.

Vegetables can also be cooked by campfire. Bake potatoes by placing around the edge of an open flame or wrapping in foil and placing near the embers. Unhusked corn can be soaked in the lake and then placed on the grate over an open flame. Other vegetables or diced potatoes can be wrapped in foil with some water and placed over hot embers.

You can make complete meals by wrapping any combination of meats and vegetables in a foil pack. Add a little seasoning, water or oil, and place over hot embers.

* Remember – Any foil you pack in, you pack out. *

Camp stove - Anytime you are cooking with a camp stove you will want to use as little fuel as possible. Following these directions will help you prepare your meals and conserve your fuel.
- Protect your stove and pots from the wind.
- When the stove is not in use, turn it off.
- Pots with lids will cook faster.
- Pots are not stable on top of a camp stove. Keep a close eye on them.
- Anytime you are stirring or adding ingredients, take the pot off the stove and place it on a firm surface.
- Mix gravies in the measured amount of cold water before adding to the pot.
- For most of your rice and soup recipes, the added ingredients can be placed in the water, or water/gravy mix, and warmed as the water is coming to a boil.
- When a recipe tells you to simmer, cover the pot and remove it from the heat. Let it sit. Simmering uses too much fuel. The dish will cook fine in hot liquid. Stir and reheat to boil every five to ten minutes until done.
- When cooking pasta, bring water to a boil, add pasta, and return to boil. Remove from heat and stir thoroughly. Cover, and let sit ten to fifteen minutes. Check to see that it's done, drain, and serve.
- Sauces and meats will have to be warmed in a separate pot.

Baking - If you decided to try to bake bread, biscuits, or dessert recipes over a campfire, here are a few suggestions.

For pan (bannock) bread and some desserts, you can use a skillet. Place the batter in a lightly oiled skillet. Place it over the fire and allow it to firm up on both sides. Now place the skillet on its edge at the front of the fire so it catches the radiant heat. Rotate

Baking in a box oven

and flip until it is done. You will need a rock to support the skillet and may need a stone to keep the bread/dessert from sliding.

You can also bake using a reflector oven. Get a nice fire with a good bed of hot embers. Place the oven slightly above and to the side of the fire. Place the batter or dough in a lightly oiled nine-inch by nine-inch baking pan. Place the pan in the oven and rotate the pan every five to ten minutes. Anytime you are baking over fire, vigilance and patience are required.

What I have related in this chapter are a bunch of different meals and ways of preparing them in the wilderness. Everyone's background is different and so, too, are our eating habits. Based on what I have told you, ideas from the outfitters websites, and your own experience, this is one area I think you can have fun with. Use your imagination, personal tastes, and culinary skills to make your own recipes. My only caution is to try new dishes at home before you take them to the wilderness.

Rich Annen

Chapter Six

Traveling in the Wilderness

Traveling in the wilderness can be as easy as you want to make it. Attitude, planning, and equipment are tangibles over which you have control. You have no control over weather, wind, and obstacles such as beaver dams, flooded portages, and deadfall. Control that which you can and prepare for that which you cannot.

At the beginning of Chapter Two, we talked about having a positive attitude and being prepared. In Chapter Three we talked about trip planning. And in Chapter Four we looked at equipment. Now let's put them together to make our travels as easy as possible.

Packing

By now you should have some idea of which packs you are going to use. The number of packs you carry will be dependent on the size of your party, the volume of each pack, and the gear you are bringing. You will also have to decide how to divide or arrange the equipment in the packs. Proper packing of each pack can make for an easier carry across a portage.

Divide up the gear into categories:
>   **Personal Gear** – Sleeping bag, pad, clothing, rain gear, etc. Gear designed for one camper's use.
>   **Camp Gear** – Tent, tarp, first-aid, etc. Gear used for the protection of the group.
>   **Cook Gear** – Stove, pots, filter, etc. Gear used to prepare sustenance for the group.
>   **Food Pack** – Edibles, for individuals or as a group.

You may be able to split different items between packs or you may want to group them by function. The object is to pack all the equipment as compactly and as efficiently as possible. Arranging the equipment in packs may be as simple as one canoe pack for a soloist or as complex as twelve packs spread between four canoes for a party of nine.

You can line your pack with a heavy plastic bag or use dry bags to keep items from getting wet. You do not want to pack items that are filled with air, so try to avoid hard-side containers. Nest pots together and fill the voids with other items such as hot pads, seasoning, dish towels, etc.

Pack heavier items close to your back and keep the weight centered from side to side. Lighter items can be packed to the outside. For frameless packs be sure something soft will be next to your back. Pack items you may need during the course of the day so they are easily accessible.

A loaded pack should not weigh more than thirty percent of your body weight. That's forty-five pounds for a 150-pound person, fifty-three pounds for a 175-pound person, or sixty-pounds for a 200-pound person. Heavy packs on rough terrain can lead to injury. Remember you are not a real voyageur; you're on vacation.

When loading a canoe, be sure it is floating and that the weight of a pack does not push it down onto rocks. The packs should sit as low as possible in the canoe. Depending on how many packs you bring, you may need to slide one of them under a thwart or the portage yoke. Medium-sized canoe packs and duffle bags have a low enough profile to do this. Smaller packs can also be placed in the bow or stern. Once a canoe is loaded, it should sit level from

Loading the canoe

bow to stern. This includes the weight of the paddlers. Position packs so they equalize the paddler's weight. Also center the packs side to side. Accomplish this by sliding a pack to the right or left or by scooting your butt over.

If you do not intend to fish while on the move, lash your fishing rod to the thwarts. Another item to lash to the thwarts is a spare paddle. One per group should be more than enough. It is like a spare tire; hopefully you will never need it.

Secure your packs to a thwart if you are heading onto a bigger lake or working against larger waves. The packs themselves will float if you capsize, but you won't need to swim around to collect them by having them connected to the canoe. The easiest way to do this is to detach one of the shoulder straps from the pack, wrap it around a thwart, and then reattach it to the pack.

If you do capsize, hang on to your paddle. Paddles are easily lost in the confusion.

Charting a Course

Each time you enter a new lake or river, become familiar with it by plotting your position on the map, looking for geographical landmarks, and checking the wind and weather conditions.

Pull out your map and compass and locate your position. Determine your direction of travel and pick out a landmark. On lakes that have peninsulas, islands, and bays, this can be challenging. Navigate these lakes in steps. Pick a landmark and paddle to it. Chart a new course with a new landmark. Continue charting and paddling until you reach your destination.

On open lakes plotting a course appears relatively easy, but on a one-mile crossing, if you are off by five degrees, you will miss your intended position by 400 feet. On these open waters, some navigators will purposely chart a course to one side of your intended destination (aim off). Once you cross the lake, you can follow the shoreline in the appropriate direction to your destination. This works well because, if your destination is not obvious, you will know which direction to travel once you reach the far shore.

Navigating by map and compass isn't all that difficult but it does require practice. The more you use a compass, the more comfortable you will become. Someone in your group should be tracking your travel at all times. You can waste a lot of time and effort chasing false bays. And where two portages are near each other, you will definitely want to pick the correct one.

Navigating on rivers and streams may appear easier. You will be following the river in the general direction you want to go. But muskegs and vegetation can create problems. Some river channels meander and picking the right course is not always easy. When seated in a canoe, you may not be able to see over the top of the vegetation. Peripheral streams or game trails may add to the confusion. Some channels have tight corners. The outside of a bend is usually deeper and faster, cut the corner and you may be grounded, go too far out, and you may be pushed into the far shore and overhanging branches.

When you can see out in front, watch for ripples in the water that will warn you of subsurface rocks or deadfall. And every now and then you will be treated to deadfall or a beaver dam blocking your route.

When you come across a beaver dam, look on either side for a portage. If none is available, look to see if there is a low area on the dam that has been used to portage canoes. Your first instinct will be to drag the canoe and gear over, but try to avoid this. Pull sideways to the dam and get out. You will find dams to be quite solid. Remove heavier packs if you have a place to set them. Maneuver the boat so it is bow first. With a person on either side, lift and set the canoe until it is across. Again, avoid dragging a loaded canoe. Reload and continue on your way.

All rapids will have portages to them. Some rapids may look navigable. If you are not familiar with the power and hydraulics of swift water, take the portage. If you are not proficient at whitewater canoeing, take the portage. If you are not familiar with these rapids, scout them, or take the portage.

Kelso River

Forecasting the Weather

Each morning, check the western sky and keep an eye on it throughout the day. The cloud formations you see can give you some idea what the weather may be like for the next few days. Most city folk have lost the art of predicting weather this way. Most assuredly the voyageurs knew how.

On most days the weather will be nonthreatening and the winds light. Then there are the rare days where heavy rain and wind will make it easy to decide it is time to hunker down and wait out the storm. In the worst conditions, your tent can be your salvation. Cozy up with a good book and let Mother Nature have a tantrum. The concern here is the other days. If the weather is threatening and the winds are picking up or gusting, what do you do?

First, determine the wind direction. In the Boundary Waters area, the weather comes from a westerly direction. But winds from an easterly direction generally mean you will get rain. Why does the storm come from the west but the winds are from the east? The upper air (prevailing) winds are from the west, pushing the fronts to the east. Lower-level winds move from high pressure to low pressure.

When a low-pressure area approaches from the west, the high-pressure area moves out to the east. Therefore, the low-level winds move from the high pressure (east) to the low pressure (west) creating an easterly wind. On the other hand, when a low-pressure area moves out to the east and high-pressure area moves in from the west, it creates a westerly wind. West is good; east is bad. Winds increase when fronts move in or out. If the winds are picking up, expect the weather to change.

Next, try to identify the cloud cover. High clouds generally indicate fair weather for the next twenty-four hours. Low clouds generally produce rain over the same period. The following are some clouds and their potential forecast:

Cirrus [L. curl] – High, thin, wispy clouds. They may develop into cirrostratus or be the leading edge of cumulonimbus. No immediate threat of rain.

Cirrostratus – Thin, high clouds that cover the entire sky, creating a hazy sunshine. Rain is a possibility within twenty-four hours.

Stratus [L. layer] – A low cloud cover blanketing the entire sky. They generally develop into nimbostratus.

Nimbostratus – Low, gray cloud blanketing the entire sky. These usually indicate that a steady rainfall is imminent, usually of a longer duration. These storms may last for hours or days.

Wilderness Canoeing - Boundary Waters

Cirrus clouds

Cumulonimbus clouds

Cumulus [L. heaped] – Low clouds formed by rising, warm, moist air. They look like cotton balls separately or loosely bunched. They produce no immediate threat of rain. In time, based on moisture and temperature, they develop into cumulus congestus.

Cumulus Congestus – Thicker clouds with flat bottoms. The tops look like cauliflower. The higher the tops are, the greater the storm threat. They may develop into Cumulonimbus. Expect rain within twenty-four hours.

Cumulonimbus – Gray cloud bottoms with tops that look like mushrooms or anvils. Expect a strong thunderstorm with lightning soon. These storms are generally short in duration but may produce heavy downpours and high winds.

Other "old school" indicators that may help with your weather forecasting include:
- o "Red sky at night, sailor's delight." A red sunset (west) indicates a dry, high-pressure system is approaching. The red is caused by dust particles in the air.
- o For the same reason the moon may appear reddish.
- o "Red sky in the morning, sailors take warning." A red sunrise (east) indicates that the high-pressure system has passed and a low-pressure storm system is approaching.
- o A bright, clear moon also indicates that high pressure has passed.
- o "Circle around the moon, rain or snow soon." A ring around the moon is caused by cirrostratus clouds. Rain is a possibility within twenty-four hours.
- o If birds are flying high, it indicates fair weather. If few birds are flying, expect rain.
- o Smell the air. If it smells earthy, swampy, or wormy, then rain is coming. Low pressure allows more odors to escape into the air.
- o Campfire smoke rising straight up means fair weather. Smoke curling means rain.

Thunderstorms

If you see lightning or hear loud thunder, find a sheltered area to wait out the storm. If you are hearing low, distant thunder, you can move. You can estimate the distance of the lightning by timing the difference between the lightning and the thunder. The speed of light is almost instantaneous. The speed of sound is about 760 mph or about 0.2 miles per second. Thus, five seconds equals one mile. Once you see the flash, start saying "one-Mississippi, two-Mississippi, etc." (or "one-thousands," or "potatoes") until you hear the thunder. Divide by five and you have your distance in miles.

By staying within fifty feet of shore, you will have some lightning protection and you can seek shelter as conditions change. Look for safe havens on the map such as campsites and portages. If you are unable to reach these areas, find an opening along the shore to land and shelter in.

Once on shore find a sheltered area and place your packs in a row. If you haven't already done so, don your rain gear. Roll the canoe over the top of the packs to keep them dry. Find a nice conifer to hunker under; I prefer cedars. Just don't pick the tallest tree on a hill top. If you have no suitable trees, pull out your tarp and slip under it.

If you are unable to get to a safe haven or cannot land in a sheltered area, look for overhanging branches along the lee shoreline.

The Federal Emergency Management Agency, or FEMA, recommends people follow the 30/30 rule: If, after seeing lightning, you cannot count to thirty before hearing thunder, seek shelter. And don't leave your sheltered area until thirty minutes after the last clap of thunder.

In a severe lightning storm, take more serious precautions. Seek shelter in a low area under a dense growth of small trees. But keep your distance from them and do not touch them. Avoid tall trees, since lightning often strikes the tallest object in an area. Follow these procedures:
- Crouch down in a catcher's position. The nearer to the ground, the less likely you will be struck.

- Roll up on the balls of your feet to minimize ground contact and place your heels together.
- Place your hands over your ears to prevent hearing damage from the thunder clap.
- Try to lower your head and elbows between your knees.
- If in a larger group, disperse so one strike does not disable your entire group.

Winds

Winds are another factor to consider when traveling. Winds produce waves. Wind will drive the waves, especially in open areas, and they will be larger on the downwind side of the lake. Sigurd Olson referred to them as "marching combers." Winds will also channel through low areas, bays, or long lakes whose length runs with the wind. Wind and waves will push your canoe around. Knowing how to handle the canoe in these conditions is critical. If you are not sure of yourself or your crew, then wait it out or you may be going for a swim in less-than-ideal conditions.

When traveling in windy conditions, determine the wind direction. Look at the tree tops and see which way and how much they are moving. Pull out your map and look for open areas, islands, peninsulas, or bays that may channel the wind or provide a break from the wind.

Look at the water. See if you can get an idea of the wave heights. Here is where binoculars come in handy. Look for white-tipped waves. This is the area you may want to avoid. Use these findings to confirm what you saw on the map. Now see if you can plot a course that minimizes your exposure to the wind and waves. If you have no wind breaks or have an open area to cross, it can still be done with caution and planning.

Wave heights of zero to one foot are of little concern. Wave heights of one to two feet are doable but a cross-wind course will be rocky; avoid it if possible. Waves greater than two feet require planning. As the Northwoods do-it-yourself expert Red Green (Steve Smith) stated: "Do not let your ego get in the way of your common sense."

As you get into these larger waves, make sure you paddle into or with the wind. If you are on a smaller lake, it is easiest to follow the shore. First follow the shoreline upwind. This gets the harder paddling out of the way and will put you into a sheltered area of the lake. It is best to paddle directly into the waves. If that's not possible, you can angle into them but keep it within thirty- to forty-five degrees or you will be struggling. As you approach the end of the lake, you will pick up a wind break from the tree line. Cut over to the other side of the lake and head downwind to your destination. Stay alert. The wind and waves will try to push your stern around so keep the thirty- to forty-five-degree rule. Maintaining speed makes steering easier when traveling downwind.

On a large lake, following the shore may not be an option. The best way to cross a lake in this situation is by tacking. Tacking is a sailing term used to describe a zigzag course to sail into the wind. In a canoe you are trying to minimize the effects of the wind. Set a course thirty to forty-five degrees into the wind. Follow it as long as you wish or until you need a break. Make a turn (come about) and set a course thirty- to forty-five-degrees downwind. Repeat until you reach your destination. Before you come about, be sure you and your partner know what to do to complete the turn and lessen your cross-wave exposure.

One thing you can do to make your crossing easier is to kneel in the boat and rest your butt on the front of your seat. This will give the boat a lower center of gravity. Another is to have both canoeists paddle on the leeward side (the side opposite the direction the waves are coming from). This will allow for more forward movement of the boat and less ruddering. When crossing a lake under these conditions, there is no time to take a break. You need to be actively paddling both into and with the wind to maintain good steerage. When crossing these windblown lakes please, please have your PFD on and secured properly.

Another skill that comes from spending time in a canoe is how to maintain your center of gravity. If you ever watched whitewater kayaking, the kayaks bounce all over the place yet the paddler's upper body remains vertical. The same applies to a canoe. Let your hips roll with the canoe but keep your upper body centered. When you paddle don't lean out, reach out. When you turn twist at the waist, don't bend. The best advice, loosen up a little.

Portaging

Before you can portage, you need to land the canoe. First, find the portage. Most are quite obvious and you will see a well-used landing with a trail running up from it. As you get into the interior, they are not as obvious and may require you to scout the area to be sure. Many a game trail has been mistaken for a portage.

If there are people at the landing, patiently wait for them to clear. If there is gear at the landing, go ahead and land but be respectful of other people's equipment. If you are at the landing and another group comes in, clear the landing and make room for them as soon as possible. Place your packs off to the side. Do the same with the canoe if you are not taking it over on your first crossing. Do not leave the canoe in the water. It may not be there when you get back.

The landings at the portages will vary. Some may be shallow with gravel or even a sandy base while others may be nothing but a stinky, muddy bottom. Or you may have a nice boulder to pull next to. And yet others may be nothing but big, jagged rocks. The rocky landings tend to be in deeper water

The first two are the easiest to land and unload. A boulder is nice but requires someone to hang on to the canoe. The rocks can be a bit of a pain. For some reason it always seems that when the wind and waves are up, it will be a rocky landing, both literally and figuratively.

When coming into a landing, determine if it is best to pull in bow first or to swing the canoe and moor sideways. The bow person has the better view and can make this call. Remember, do not beach the canoes. Pull in until the bow barely touches the lake bed. The stern paddler can steady the canoe until the bow paddler exits. Steady the canoe by placing your paddle horizontal to the side with your flattened blade tip about a foot underwater. This will allow the bow paddler to exit and then stabilize the boat from shore.

The canoe can be floated in a little to allow for a shallower exit by the stern paddler. DO NOT lift the bow of the boat when you are floating it in; the canoe will lose its stability and it may tip over. I have seen this happen a few times and everyone finds it funny except for the guy and gear in the water.

If you moor sideways the boat will have to be steadied so either paddler can exit. You can do this by wedging your paddle on the lake bottom and levering in on the top to hold the boat to the shore. If you are in deeper water this may not work. If so, see if there is something on shore to grab on to or use the method described above.

Unloading in shallow water is usually easy. Both canoers can grab a pack as they exit the boat. The canoe will usually behave and stay where it's at. On rocky landings or if waves are present, one canoer will have to tend the canoe while the other unloads. If you are near fast water, keep an eye on the canoe at all times.

When you unload you should have a plan. Who is responsible for which packs and who is responsible for the canoe? This will make unloading and the portages go easier. We alternate who portages the canoe so everyone can enjoy this pleasure. The crew of each canoe should be responsible to portage all the gear in their canoe.

How many trips you make across a portage is your choice. We generally do ours in two trips. When crossing an unfamiliar portage, I prefer to do the first crossing with a pack so I can scout the terrain. For short portages, twenty rods or less, you can use a two-person carry. First, place the heavier packs on your backs. You can leave a light pack in the canoe if you must, but place it near the bow or stern. One person is on one side of the bow and the other person is on the other side of the stern. Lift and carry the canoe across, switching sides as your arms get tired. On portages of fifty rods or less, ones that we are familiar with, we may double pack and make the crossing in one trip.

For longer portages, 150 rods or longer, we use a staging method the voyageurs referred to as "poses" [L. stop, pause]. This method also can be used on shorter portages. On the first leg travel about five minutes or fifty rods. Set your pack to the side and return to the landing. Grab another pack or the canoe and travel ten minutes or 100 rods. Set the pack/canoe off to the side. Return to where you left your first pack. Take this pack ten minutes or 100 rods. Set the pack off to the side and return to the pack/canoe. Repeat until you reach the far landing. By using this method, you get breaks and these longer portages won't be as trying.

If you enjoy wildlife, the portage is where you will see much of it. It's kind of hard when you have a canoe overhead, but keep your eyes open and your camera ready when you are carrying a pack or on the return trip. Loading the canoe is similar to unloading and will be dependent on the landing. Be sure the canoe is floating as you load it and check to be sure you have all your gear before you shove off.

You will experience obstacles on almost every portage:

Wet lands – You will be going through low areas that are wet, even in dry weather. You can try and skirt these mud puddles, as others have, but sometimes it's safer to go through the middle. Be careful; some of the mud can suck your shoes off.

Rock fields – You are on the Canadian Shield. There are plenty of rocks you will have to pick your way through. Be careful when stepping on rocks; some can be loose or slippery.

Boulders – Not rocks, boulders. You may encounter some large boulders that block your path. You simply have to climb over them.

Deadfall – Recently fallen trees can block a portage requiring you to bushwhack around it. For smaller trees you may be better off using your saw to clear the trail. Some deadfall may have already been delimbed by previous travelers, leaving just the trunk. You can climb over it or crawl under it, whichever looks easiest.

Beaver ponds – Industrious critters, aren't they? I was waist deep in one between Lower Pauness and Shell. On the deeper ones, it is better to float your gear across in the canoe. In some low areas boards or boardwalks have been placed to ease the impact of you slogging through these areas. Unfortunately, when the water is high, some of these boards will float. Stepping from one floating board to the next reminds me of the Donkey Kong game of old.

Rivers / Streams – If you are traveling along a river system you will encounter portages that may follow the shoreline of the river to avoid rapids or shallow water. These portages may have you walking on loose river rock. Yet on others you may find yourself fording a stream or two.

Elevation change – You will be up and down often. You can check the lake elevations on the map. This will give you the elevation change between the lakes. But that doesn't reflect the actual elevation changes of the portage. By reading the topographical

Deadfall

lines on the map, you can get an idea of how many times and how much the elevation changes on each portage.

Overhead obstacles – Make a mental note of any overhead obstructions. You may be able to walk under them when carrying a pack, but it's a different story with a canoe. You only have to nail an obstruction once with a canoe to drive the point home. You will be more observant in the future.

Foliage – In the less-traveled areas, you may find the portages overgrown with brush or grass. It may be easier to feel your way with your feet.

Wildlife – Most wildlife will beat a hasty retreat. Some may require a little encouragement. And some, mainly moose, really don't care about moving out of your way. You'll just have to wait them out.

With all the obstacles and potential problems I have listed, it seems as though I am being a pessimist. Not true. I just want to give you a heads up so if any problems arise, you can handle them without any difficulty and enjoy your time spent in the wilderness.

We have spent much time in the wilderness and have met and overcome most of the challenges one can imagine. We still come to the Boundary Waters and we still enjoy our trips.

Chapter Seven

Establishing Your Camp

A fter a wonderful day of travel and exploration, it is time to kick back and relax. First you need to find a campsite. In your planning you should have noted a few sites on the map as possibilities. Campsites in the more popular areas, or those within a few hours of the entry points, are used more than those in other areas. Therefore, getting your preferred site may not be a possibility so keep other sites in mind. It is best to look for sites early in the afternoon when traveling in these areas.

Not all sites are created equal. Some sites will offer a comfortable gathering area around the fire grate or a nice swim area. Others may have a carpet of pine straw on which to walk and sleep, while others will offer magnificent views. Some may even offer all of the above. In the more popular areas, sites may have been expanded and improved. In contrast if you travel to the interior, the sites are used less, are generally smaller, and the tent pads are a bit more rustic.

Where and when you camp is somewhat dependent on the type of trip you are taking. For short trippers you may have to settle for what's available. Don't despair; this is a beautiful area. The voyageur-style trippers usually settle for what's convenient. If you are a base camper, you will want to find something nicer since you will be spending some time there. If you get a late start, find a site that will work for the first night. The next day you can spend more time looking for a more suitable site.

You are on the Canadian Shield and there will be rocks. Some of the large rock formations will offer you a front porch to sit on and look out over the lake. Others will offer you a nice fishing pier.

Setting up Camp

Once you have selected a site, it is time to set up camp. Unload your canoes and secure them by bringing them out of the water. Look for a sheltered area close to the water where they can be stored until needed. You do not want to leave canoes in the water. They can get beat up on the rocks or go missing.

Sleeping tents have priority. Survey the site and determine where the tent(s) will go. Tent areas are usually well established. Almost all sights will have two spots that have been used for tents; some may have as many as four. Most tent pads are set back and sheltered. Use the available spots; do not hack a new area for your tent. Pick a spot with the fewest rocks and roots and check overhead for "widow makers." Widow makers are dead trees or branches that have the potential to fall, or those that have already fallen and are leaning against another tree. A strong wind may bring them down. You do not want to be under them.

When it comes time to pound in your tent stakes, don't be surprised if they don't go in. Remember, you are on the Canadian Shield. You can put a stake or a stick sideways through the tent loop and weight down the ends with rocks. Most tents will be fine without all the stakes in, just keep your eyes on it if the wind picks up. Once your tent is up, throw your sleeping bag, clothes, and sleeping pad in the tent. If you have a self-inflating mattress pad, open the valve so it can inflate. The clothing you are not wearing to bed can be used as a pillow. Throw them in a stuff sack and wrap them in your towel for comfort.

Next, find an area where you can do your cooking. You will want a relatively flat spot for the stove. You could use the top of the fire grate but your cooking may conflict with your campfire. You can flip a canoe upside down and place two six-inch-diameter logs under each end to stabilize it. The canoe bottom provides a large, flat area for cooking and serving. Use caution if you choose to cook on a composite or plastic canoe.

Or you may choose to put your kitchen in a protected area. Look for a spot under trees. Find a flat area on the ground to put your stove and clear away all dried vegetation. Use a PFD or your camp seat to kneel on when cooking. Keep the wind off of the stove by using the tarp, packs, or reflector oven as a wind break. By doing this the food will cook faster and you will save fuel.

Now it's time to put up a tarp. Tarps are optional. If the weather forecast is clear you can leave it in the pack. You may even choose not to bring one along. On other days it may be the first item you deploy when you come into camp. The tarp will provide protection for you and your packs during storms. You can also use it as a wind break. I prefer to put mine over the kitchen. It keeps me dry when I'm cooking.

We always carry a twelve-foot by twelve-foot tarp with lines attached at the corners and four stakes rolled up inside. There are numerous ways to hang the tarp depending on what's available.

As a rainfly you can:
- Suspend the tarp by tying the four corners to four trees.
- Suspend the tarp by tying two corners to two trees and use paddles for the other two corners.
- In a treeless area, use four paddles.
- You can string a cord between two trees and drape the tarp over it. Use paddles on the four corners.
- Stake or tie down the two back corners and tie the front corners to two trees or use paddles.

As a wind break you can:
- Tie the tarp vertically between two trees, much like a sail.
- Use a tree as a center post. Place the middle of the tarp against the tree. Fan out the sides. Stake the bottom corners. Tie the top corners to trees or use paddles.
- Stake or tie down the two front corners. Tie the two back corners to two trees or use paddles

There are only a few minor items left to address and you will be set for the evening. If you haven't done so already, scout out a path to the latrine. Getting to some latrines can be interesting and some may even offer a view. We place the potty pack at the start of the path. It contains toilet paper and antibacterial wipes. If the pack is gone, the latrine is being used.

Next establish the watering hole. This is an area along the shore where you can fetch water without getting your feet wet. Look for large rocks in the water that you can step on. The water should be at least a foot deep so you won't stir up sediment when you dip your pot in. When getting water first skim the surface with the bottom of the pot. This will remove some of the debris and pollen that may be floating on top. Once the watering hole is established, tell the rest of the group where it is so no one bathes or rinses their socks there.

For convenience we use a water bladder and hang it from a tree. Fill the bladder with lake water, attach the pump filter to the bottom hose and drinking water is readily available. I do not recommend gravity filters. As they get dirty, they run slowly and some cannot be field cleaned.

Lastly, string a clothesline so wet clothing can be hung to dry. Smaller groups can get by with just tent and tarp cords or even tree branches, but larger groups usually need more hanging space.

You are now set up. Put on some dry clothes, take a swim or go fishing. Or you can get your camp seat out and find a place to sit. You can even rearrange the rustic furniture around the fire grate. It's time to wind down and reflect on the day. It's happy hour, wilderness-style. Appetizers anyone?

Wilderness Canoeing - Boundary Waters

Tarp shelter from the rain

Happy hour, wilderness-style

Campfires

If you want a campfire, find some firewood. There should be some next to the grate, but it probably will only be enough to get a fire started. Grab your saw and compass and pick a direction that looks good. Note the direction you are heading and which direction gets you back to camp, just in case you get turned around. If you are at a site that is used often, you may have to travel a little farther afield. If you camped on a small island, you may have to go canoeing to find firewood.

Use only deadfall or dead trees. Do not cut live trees; they won't burn anyway. You're in a forest. There's dead wood all around. When you find a dead tree, cut off a branch and drag it back to camp. A few of these should be enough for the night. Avoid felling standing dead trees as bad things can happen. Once in camp break or cut the branches into foot-long pieces. I usually divide mine into kindling, small fuel, and large fuel.

Next you will need some tinder. Use shredded paper or cardboard from food packaging or look for anything dry: pine needles, cedar leafs, deciduous leafs, or duff (dry vegetation covering the ground). Place the tinder in the fire grate. If you are using a fire stick, place it in the middle of the tinder. Build a covering of twigs over the top of the tinder, leaving a small window to insert a lit match. In damp weather you may choose to add a little Boy Scout water to the kindling.

Once the tinder and kindling are burning, add progressively larger pieces of firewood until you establish a good bed of hot embers. Keep the fire small and within the fire grate. Smaller fires are safer and require less wood to maintain. As the night winds down, stop feeding the fire and watch as it dies. In dry or windy weather, douse the remaining embers with water. In the next chapter we will talk about more primitive ways of starting a fire.

Cooking

If you are going to cook over the fire, you will have to build and bank the fire dependent on what you are cooking. If you are going to cook using the stove, find a flat spot as described earlier. Set up a work area with all your cooking equipment at hand. Have a flat area next to the stove or campfire to set your pot on when stirring or adding ingredients. Water for meals can be taken from the lake, just be sure you boil the water to sterilize both the water and the pot.

If you cooked pasta you will need to drain it. You can bring a pot strainer or place and hold the lid on loosely. When draining the pasta, follow the 150-feet-from-camp/water rule. Do not drain the pasta in the lake. Any loose noodles seem to fluoresce as they sit on the lake bottom.

Now select your entrée and follow the recipe directions along with the cooking procedures from Chapter Five.

Clean-up

Once you have finished and everyone has eaten, it's time to clean up. Leaving dirty dishes out is an invitation for critters to come into your campsite. Any leftovers need to be placed in a plastic bag and packed out. Do not dump them in the fire or the latrine.

Here is a way to get things clean and keep them relatively free of bacteria.
- Add a little lake water to your cook pot and scrub it.
- Dump the water 150 feet away from the lake or streams and not in the latrine.
- Fill a pot half full of lake water, cover, and bring to a boil. Transfer the hot water to the second pot, cover, and return the water to a boil.
- Remove from heat and pour an equal amount of the hot water in both pots.
- Add a drop of dish soap to one of the pots and throw in the scrub pad while the water is still hot. You now have reasonably sterile wash and rinse pots.
- Once the water has cooled, wash the cookware, mess kits, and utensils.
- Dump the soapy water 150 feet from any lake or streams.
- Rinse the soap from the wash pot with water from the rinse pot.

Securing the Camp

There are a few minor items to check and a couple important tasks to perform before you turn in. Most of them you will want to do before dark.

Take a walk around the camp and be sure the canoes are in a safe area and flipped over. Check tent, tarp, and clothes lines to be sure they are tight. Remove any items you will need for the evening, then place your pack under the tarp or place it in the plastic bag you used as a pack liner. Pack or consolidate any other equipment and place it under the tarp. In heavy weather drop the tarp to cover the gear. Place the paddles and a few rocks on the tarp to prevent the wind from catching it.

The Forest Service recommends putting all remaining food in the food pack. Collect any non-burnable trash and place it in a plastic bag. Place this bag and the leftover food bag, if any, in the food pack. Secure your food pack. The Forest Service recommends you suspend your pack between two trees. Hoist the pack so it is ten feet off the ground and six feet from either tree. You will need two trees and two ropes to do this.

Another method is to find a tree with a stout branch. Throw your rope so it drapes the branch six feet from the tree. Hoist your pack until it is ten feet off the ground. This method only uses one rope.

To suspend a pack ten feet off of the ground, you will need to get your rope over a fifteen- to twenty-foot-high branch. You can coil the rope and toss it, but that rarely works. You can tie a heaving hitch on the coil so it deploys only when it is over the branch and on its way down. Or, better, grab one of the stuff sacks and put a few smooth rocks in it. Tie a clove hitch around the neck of the bag. Now toss or swing the sack over the branch. No matter which method you use, it's fun to watch. Attach a rope to the food pack with a carabiner or a good knot. Hoist the pack until it is ten feet off the ground. You can use a paddle to help push the pack up as you pull on the line. Tie the haul line to an adjoining tree.

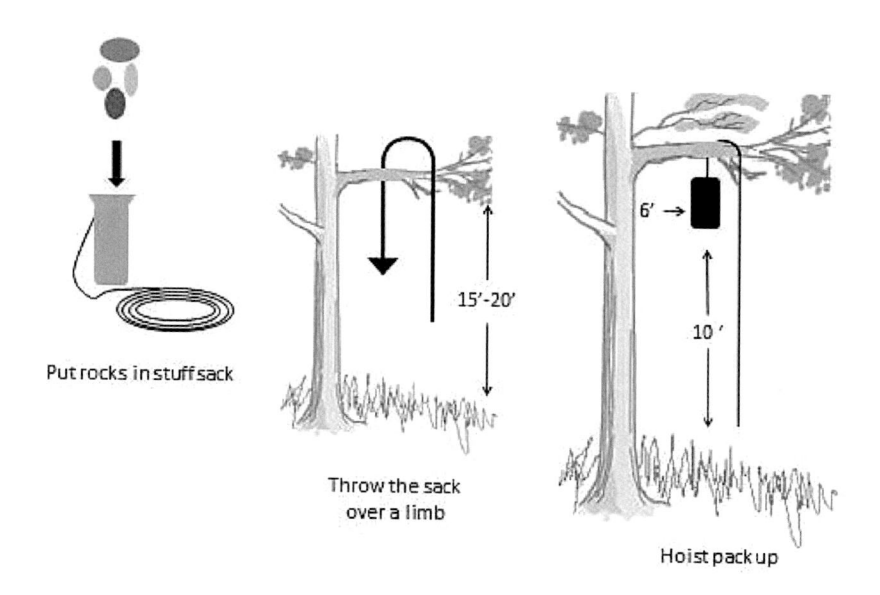

Put rocks in stuff sack

Throw the sack over a limb

Hoist pack up

Hanging your food bag

Most campers will use the same, most-convenient tree for hanging their food. Bears can become wise to this. Cliff Jacobson, wilderness author and consultant, recommends "break the classical conditioning habit by grounding food packs in an unexpected place. ... One solution is to take food packs out of the camp area, well away from hiking trails, game paths, and human traffic. Be sure to seal your food in plastic so there are no odors."

Bear-proof containers are another option and are becoming more popular. They are required in some National Parks. They are effective but they can get bulky. Bears have been known to carry them off so you might want to tether the container to a tree.

Over the years we have been in areas where hanging the food pack is not an option. Since we do not use bear-proof containers, we have had to get creative. One method is to suspend the pack over a rock face. Keep the pack ten feet from the ground and well below the top of the rock.

The method we use the most is the canoe vault. Place a canoe upright on the ground, set the food pack inside, then nestle an upside-down canoe on top of the other canoe. Use your rope to secure the two together. Some experts may disagree and say we are toying with the potential for a shredded canoe. We have used this method dozens of times and have had no intrusions of any kind. Even the little critters stay away.

There is no foolproof (bear-proof) method of protecting your food in the wilderness. There are stories of bears opening bear-proof containers, of chewing through hanging rope, and of going out on branches and hoisting up your pack.

All the methods I have listed are deterrents. The harder it is for bears to get to the food, the less likely they are to try. Bears are quick learners and stupid campers teach them where to get easy food. If a bear comes into camp and threatens your food, scare them off by banging pots, waving your arms, and yelling. Camp-wise bears can become a nuisance. Repeat offenders are often euthanized (a nice way of saying executed). Save a bear. Keep a clean camp.

Now that you have everything locked down, it's time to enjoy the sunset and the warmth of the fire. Have a great conversation

Canoe vault

with family and friends. Relive the day's adventure. Have a cigar, or a sip of bourbon, or both. And let the loons serenade you.

Before you turn in, your last responsibility is the fire. Be sure there is no way that fire can go beyond the fire box. Watch it burn out or douse it. There are tragic personal stories of people who were the cause of major forest fires because of a campfire that was not properly extinguished.

Breaking Camp

Hopefully you had a pleasant night, are well-rested and ready for another adventurous day. As you take down and pack up your equipment, there are a few things to consider.

Be sure the fire is out and the embers are cold. If not, douse the embers until they are. Stir the ashes and remove any trash you or any others may have thrown in and pack it out. Leave a pile of wood beside the fire grate for the next group. Even on the off chance there was none there when you came, leave some as you go out.

Lastly take a walk through the entire camp. Pick up bits of trash that may have dropped or were overlooked. For you smokers, cigarette butts are trash whether on the ground or in the fire grate. Be sure none of your equipment is forgotten. As you leave the campsite, there should be no evidence of your stay. Get in the habit of using sound **"Leave No Trace"** practices.

Chapter Eight

Activities

In our modern society, people are active or are entertained most of the day or night. Many are involved with outdoor activities, but far too many are dependent on computers and television for their entertainment. These items are not available in the wilderness. When you are traveling, your day is filled with plenty of entertaining activities and sights. Once you have established camp, what do you do? By far the favorite activity is fishing, but there are many other things to do.

Top of my list is to kick back and enjoy the sights and sounds. Grab your camp seat and head toward the lake. Find a nice sunny spot and get comfy. Bring your binoculars, and don't forget your camera. I also bring a book. If nothing is happening on the lake or in the air, I can turn to my book. Always keep an ear to the sounds of nature.

Or take a swim. It's helpful and refreshing to rinse off the day's dust or to cool off on a hot day. Before you do any cliff diving, be sure to scout the waters below for rocks and deadfall. Summers are short and many of the lakes are deep, so a quick dip may be all you will want.

Fishing

Fishing is one of the reasons many come to this area. I won't lie to you. Fishing is not one of my strengths. Even though I fish, I am only a student of the sport. I dutiful listen as I try to make sense of what others are saying.

Each lake is unique in its structure, depth, and type of fish. Each fish species reacts differently to the seasons, lures, and baits. Talk to those who are knowledgeable of the area as your first step. Outfitters or local bait shops will usually give you good advice, or go online and find fishing websites and blogs for the area. Go to setthehook.com for tackle suggestions or try bwca.com and page down to "Forums/Message boards" to discuss a variety of fish-related topics.

You can also go online and review the lakes you will be traveling through or staying on. For Minnesota lakes, go to dnr.state.mn.us and click on "Fishing," then "Lake Finder." You will need to know which county the lake is in (St. Louis, Cook, or Lake). Explore the site. It has a number of add-on maps. For Quetico lakes go to mnr.gov.on.ca and click on "Fishing" then "Fish ON-line." You can take a tutorial or click "Try Fish ON-line" to go directly to the site.

You need a license if you are going to fish. Purchase one at the outfitters, a bait shop, or online. To purchase a Minnesota license, go to dnr.state.mn.us. To purchase a Canadian license, go to mnr.gov.on.ca. You will also need an Outdoors Card in Canada. If you purchased online at either site, be sure to review or print the applicable rules. When fishing in Canada, remember artificial bait only and barbless or pinched-down hooks.

The more popular fish in the Boundary Waters area are walleye, smallmouth bass, northern pike, and lake trout, with walleye being the favorite.

There are as many ways to fish as there are fishermen. Shore fishing is quick and easy but going out in the canoe is generally more productive. Below is a compilation of some of the suggested fishing spots and lures mentioned by various outfitters and fishermen.

Walleye – Look for walleye near moving water or along points, spits, or over gravel beds. In the spring look for them in five to fifteen feet of water. In the summer they go a little deeper, ten to thirty feet of water. Try floating plugs (Rapala), spinners (Mepps), lindy rigs, or walking sinkers. Get your lure down in the five- to ten-foot range. Try jigging with just a leech or a crawler on your hook. On rocky points or gravel shoals, use a bottom bouncer or a jig head with a crawler or leech. Walleyes are light sensitive and fishing is best in the morning and evening.

Smallmouth Bass – Look for bass in shallow areas and along protected shorelines and bays. Fish the edge of fallen trees or weed beds, or along spits, shoals, or submerged rocks. Use spinners (Mepps) or jigs with crawlers. On calmer days try top-water plugs or poppers. If these don't work, try a diving plug.

Northern Pike – Pike can be found in the spring near moving water, in shallow bays, or around islands and points. In the summer look for them in five to fifteen feet of water near submerged structures such as logs or rocks, over drop offs, or along weed beds. Try using large spoons, spinners, rattlers, and plugs. Pike are an aggressive fish with teeth. Use a steel leader and be careful when handling them. Many fishermen release pike because they do not want to deal with the Y bones. In smaller pike this can be true, but for larger ones they are dealt with rather easily. The best way to learn is watch someone do it or query it online. YouTube has some good instructional clips.

Lake Trout – Lake trout prefer cold, clear water, 45°F to 55°F. The best way to fish them is by trolling. Use one- to two-ounce sinkers to get your trolling rig down to the depth you want. In the spring run your rig at twenty to thirty feet. In the summer try thirty to forty feet. Use a variety of large spoons and plugs to attract them.

Trying to decide what bait or tackle to bring can be, well, trying. Carrying and caring for live minnows is something I don't prefer. Some opt for leeches or night crawlers, which are a bit easier to manage. Once again check with your bait shop or outfitter. Or you can try some of the scented baits. Gulp and Yum are two of the more popular.

Appendix 10 has a list of suggested tackle. Remember you will be carrying this equipment over portages so keep it small. Limit your tackle to the fish species you intend to fish. Leave the lead sinkers at home; they poison and kill the loons who may accidently ingest them.

Now that you have caught your fish, what do you do? While still away from camp, look along the shoreline for an accessible area that has a reasonably flat rock. Gut and filet your fish on top of the flat rock or the blade of your paddle. Rinse the filets in clear lake water and place in a plastic bag. Toss the guts and bones as far back in the woods as you can. Once in camp prepare your fish to your liking. If you catch your fish while in camp, go ahead and clean them near shore. Rinse the area and toss the guts and bones in the woods well away from camp.

Exploring

If you are on a voyageur-style trip, you're already exploring. You can plan your route to include specific lakes or rivers, waterfalls, pictographs, or geological features. If you are a base camper, you can take day trips to the various sights.

Waterfalls — Many of the larger waterfalls and cascades are marked on the maps, but there are lots of smaller ones that are not. Keep your eyes and ears open. Some may be a short hike from the portages while others can only be seen from the lake. The Basswood River Falls along the border and the Falls Chain in southeastern Quetico are some of the grandest. All of the falls offer photo opportunities.

Pictographs — One of the most intriguing sights for me is the Native American / First Nation pictographs. Pictographs are ancient paintings found on cave or rock walls. The paintings in the Boundary Waters area date back 300 to 400 years. They are believed to have been painted by the Ojibwe, though some of the older ones may have been by the Cree. The paints were created using fish oil or bear fat mixed with an iron oxide and a glue from ground sturgeon cartilage.

The sites where these paintings appear are believed to be special or, perhaps, sacred. The reason for the paintings may be a coming-of-age vision, a depiction of a dream, or part of a vision quest sought by a shaman. Most of the figures are creatures

Eddy / Knife Falls

common to the natives such as bears, elk, moose, caribou, and hares. You will also find human figures, canoes, and some abstract symbols. Some also depict the native spirits (manitous) such as the Thunderbird, Missikenabek (the Great Horned Serpent), Missepishu (the Great Lynx), or a mamaygwessey, a small mythical creature.

The mamaygwessey's features are a round head, no nose, six fingers and six toes. They live in the rocks along rapids and lake shores. They get their fun by moving or hiding items in camp and may even upset canoes

Rich Annen

or set them adrift. Most unexplainable incidents are blamed on the mamaygwessey.

There are roughly a dozen documented pictograph sites in the Boundary Waters and twice that many in the Quetico. It is assumed there are many more yet to be discovered. Part of the fun is trying to find them. Few of these sites are marked on maps.

The best way to locate the known sites is with Michael Furtman's book, *Magic on the Rocks*. He gives you a background on the people who drew the paintings, the types of images, and detailed directions on how to find them.

Geological Formations - You are traveling on the Canadian Shield, possibly on the Duluth Complex or on the Laurentian Divide. Maybe even in the Misquah Hills. There are many geological formations. Very few are marked on maps. Watch for the granite cliffs along the Kawishiwi River, Kekekabic Lake, Knife Lake, Lac La Croix, and many others.

Hiking - Depending on where you travel or camp, you may be able to take a short hike. Many of the lakes and portages have access to the hiking trails. A short hike on one of these trails will take you to the interior of the forest. I know some will think I am silly, but if you have never been to the depths of a large forest it is worth it. It will give you a whole new perspective of the wilderness. Remember to bring your compass and day pack with your essentials. Some of the major hiking trails that traverse the Boundary Waters are the Kekekabic, Snowbank-Old Pines, Border Route, and Sioux-Hustler.

Photography

We have talked about all the different sights you will see: the wildlife, waterfalls, the landscape, sunsets, and the serenity of the lakes along with the time spent with friends and family. Photography is a great way to preserve those memories. You do not have to bring expensive cameras; the digital, pocket ones work well. Sony and Olympus have some for around $100. Most will also have a video setting to add more documentation to your trip.

I carry a pocket camera with a 4 GB memory card. This allows me about 200 pictures, fewer if I shoot video. A fully charged battery at the start will last for a five- to six-day trip, but you might want to bring a backup battery just in case. I would caution you on bringing your smart phone for picture taking. As stated before you will probably not have reception and you will be in a wet environment. It's not worth risking your $500 phone.

Another option is to bring a video camera. There are a number of smaller ones for about $300. I use a Sony Handycam. You'll need a 16 GB memory card and a backup battery when you start shooting video.

If you are really into photography or videography, this is a great place to use your skills. Larger, more complex cameras and lenses will take far better-quality pictures than pocket cameras. Consider a small tripod for shots around camp or a clamp-on mount for video on the go. GoPro has a variety of cameras and mounts. Every year there is a contest for the best Boundary Waters photo. If interested, go to bwca.com to enter or just to see some great photos.

All of this equipment is electronic and, therefore, sensitive to moisture. You will need to protect your equipment. Dry bags work great. If, by chance, your camera does become damp, do not pack it in the dry bag. Once sealed there is nowhere for the moisture to go but into your camera. Place a moisture-absorbing packet or a handful of rice in a cloth bag and add it to your open storage bag.

Bird Watching

Many people enjoy watching and identifying the numerous birds you will encounter in the Boundary Waters area. I was never much of a bird watcher and, for the most part, can only identify the more common ones. On a trip to Isle Royale with my niece and her husband, both very accomplished and educated ornithologists, I was schooled on the various birds we came across. My niece and her husband could identify any of the birds by sight or call. They would also call to the birds and get responses. This continued the length of the Greenstone Trail. Since then I have developed a better appreciation for birds.

I had a similar experience with another niece, a biologist, while tide pooling along the California coastline. She was able to identify any and all of the sea creatures we found. It adds a lot to a trip when you can tour with experts.

While you are on the water, look for loons, mergansers, and other ducks. Watch overhead for eagles, turkey vultures, and perhaps an osprey. While on portages or in camp, you will see any number of birds including sparrows, warblers, chickadees, nuthatches, or thrushes. Listen for their various calls or, my favorite, the serenade of a loon.

A good reference book is *Canoe Country Wildlife*, by Mark Stensaas. For more detailed information, look to *National Geographic Field Guide to the Birds of North America* or *The Sibley Field Guide to Birds of Eastern North America*.

Night Sky

Stargazing has been around forever, but it takes on a new meaning in the clear skies of the Northwoods. The glow of city lights, even in some rural areas, will outshine many of the weaker stars. Once you are away from the city, the stars almost pop out of the sky. On some nights they seem close enough to touch. It's no wonder why the ancients kept watch on the skies.

Locating Constellations - Most of us are familiar with the common constellations we learned as a child: the Big Dipper and Little Dipper, Orion's Belt, and the North Star (Polaris). Some of you may be more knowledgeable about the stars. The rest of us will need a book or chart. Go to your local book store or go online to find one that fits your needs. While searching for these books, see if they have a sky chart or a planisphere. These charts can be adjusted by hemisphere, date, and time. It makes viewing easier.

When trying to look at the sky map/chart and the stars, use a dim light. A bright white light will ruin your night vision. A red light/lens works best. If you are in a group, and especially if you're with children, use a tight-beamed flashlight. This beam can be used as a pointer to locate the stars and constellations. Before you go, learn how to quickly locate Polaris without the aid of a chart.

Meteors - Another phenomenon you may see are meteor showers. Meteor showers are caused by meteoroids entering the earth's atmosphere. Meteoroids are debris left by comets. The comet's orbital path eventually becomes filled with this debris. As the earth orbits the sun, it passes through these comet trails causing meteor showers. Since the earth's orbit and the comet's orbit are predictable, so are the meteor showers. Depending on the size of the trail, these showers can last for days or weeks. Below are some to watch for:

- Eta Aquarids – Trail from Halley's Comet. Visible from April 21 to May 20, peaking around May 6. Visible in the predawn hours in the western sky.
- June Bootids – Trail from Pons-Winnecke Comet. Visible from June 26 to July 2, peaking around June 27. Visible in the predawn hours in the western sky.
- Perseids – Trail from Swift-Tuttle Comet. Visible from July 17 to August 24, peaking around August 12. Visible in the predawn hours in the northern sky.

In August of 2015, while camping on Ima Lake, we were treated to the largest meteor I have ever seen. It looked like a huge bottle rocket and I swear I heard a whooshing sound as it passed overhead. A friend of mine was camping at the same time on Isle Royale with a scout group and witnessed the same meteor, approximately 120 miles east of us.

Aurora Borealis - The Northern Lights have always fascinated man. The earliest human (Cro-Magnon) documentation of the Aurora came from cave paintings dating back to 30,000 BC. The Chinese first wrote of the Aurora in 2600 BC. The Aurora Borealis was named by Galileo Galilea in 1619. "Aurora" after the Roman Goddess of the dawn and "Boreas" from the Greek name for the north wind.

Native and First Nation tribes had many explanations for the Northern Lights. Most considered them the dancing spirits of deceased animals or loved ones. It was believed that the brighter

Aurora Borealis

and more active the lights, the happier the spirits. The Cree referred to them as "the dance of the spirits," and the North American Inuit believe them to be the spirits playing football (soccer) with a walrus head.

The lights are caused by electrically charged particles that were ejected from the sun. Most of us know this as sun spots; the learned call them coronal mass ejections. The lights are caused when these particles contact the earth's magnetic fields at both the north and south poles. The Southern Lights are called Aurora Australis.

The greater the sun activity, the greater the light show. The lights glow primarily green but may show red, blue, pink, and purple. These lights are more visible the further north you are, but during high activity they may be seen as far south as the lower United States. Go to gi.alaska.edu/AuroraForecast to see how active the lights will be.

Practice Survival Skills

Navigation - How to navigate without a map or compass is a survival skill you should practice. There are various scenarios that could happen that would leave you without either.

You first need to orient yourself. There are many ways to do this. You can use an ordinary dial watch as a compass. If all you have is a digital watch, it can still be done by laying out a watch face on the ground. Or you can use a shadow stick to determine east and west. You can even use vegetation to determine direction.

For ordinary dial watches:
- Take off your watch and lay it on a flat surface.
- Point the hour hand at the sun. In the summer, during daylight savings time (CDT), you will use the 1 o'clock position as a reference; in the winter, during standard time (CST), you will use the 12 o'clock position as a reference.
- North can be found halfway between the hour hand and the 1 or 12 o'clock positions.
- Go left (counterclockwise) of the hour hand in the a.m.; go right (clockwise) of the hour hand in the p.m.
- Determine your direction of travel and establish a landmark.
- Put your watch back on.

For digital watches:
- Clear an area on the ground.
- Poke a stick upright in the ground.
- Locate the tip of the stick's shadow and use it as the center of the clock face.
- Draw or imagine a clock face.
- Use the shadow line as the hour hand.
- Locate the 1 (CDT) or 12 (CST) o'clock position.
- North can be found halfway between the hour hand and the 1 or 12 o'clock positions.
    - Go left (counterclockwise) of the hour hand in the a.m.; go right (clockwise) of the hour hand in the p.m.
- Determine your direction of travel and establish a landmark.

If you have no watch, use a shadow stick to determine an east-west line.
- Clear an area on the ground.
- Poke a stick upright in the ground.
- Place another stick or a pebble at the tip of the shadow.
- Repeat placing a stick or pebble at the tip of the shadow every twenty to thirty minutes.
- The sticks or pebbles will form an east / west line.
- Remember the sun is southerly. Therefore, with the shadow pointing away from you, west will be to your left.
- Determine your direction of travel and establish a landmark.

Other less accurate ways of determining direction is from the vegetation. Leaves tend to grow toward the sun, which would be in a southerly direction. Pine needles tend to grow with the wind so they may point in a north-northeasterly direction. Moss is said to grow on the north side of a tree (but it also grows on the swamp side and sometimes all around a tree).

As night falls there are more ways to get your bearings. Sunsets are westerly, sunrises easterly. By far the best way to re-establish your bearings is by the stars, primarily the North Star (Polaris). To locate Polaris, find the Big Dipper (Ursa Major), the Little Dipper (Ursa Minor), or Cassiopeia. From the Big Dipper locate the two stars that make up the ladle end of the constellation. Draw a line through these stars and out about five times the depth of the ladle to Polaris. From the Little Dipper follow the handle to the last star, which is Polaris.

Cassiopeia is on the opposite side of Polaris than the Big Dipper. In the summer the Big Dipper is easier to find in the evening, but in the early morning hours it may be hidden by the horizon. By identifying Cassiopeia, you can then locate Polaris. Cassiopeia will look like a 3 when rising and an M when overhead. If you draw a line that bisects the bottom valley of the 3 or the right side valley of the M, that line will point toward Polaris.

Telling Time

So you have a compass but no watch. How can you tell time? Easy ... use a stick or your paddle as a sundial. Here is how you can estimate the time of day.

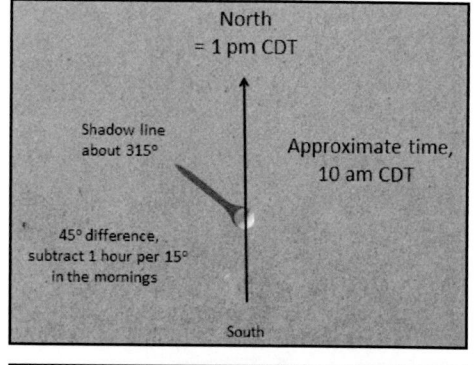

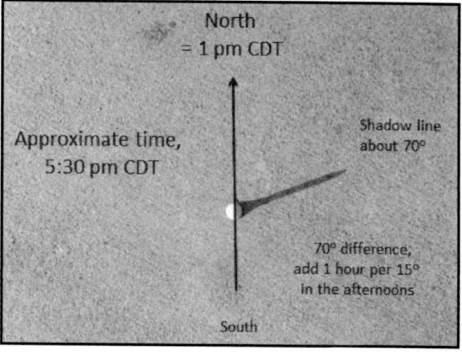

Draw a line on the ground that runs north and south. Place a stick at the south end of the line. Use your compass to determine how many degrees east or west of north the shadow falls. Each hour will equal fifteen degrees (360 degrees divided by twenty-four hours equals fifteen degrees per hour). North (360 degrees) will be 1 pm CDT. If the shadow falls at 315 degrees, it is a forty-five-degree difference. Subtract one hour for every fifteen degrees in the mornings. One p.m. minus three hours equals 10 a.m. If the shadow falls at seventy degrees, it is a seventy-degree difference. Add one hour for every fifteen degrees in the evenings. One p.m. plus four and a half hours equals 5:30 p.m.

You can use the same procedure while on the water. Face the bow of your canoe north. The stern paddler holds their paddle vertical. Estimate the degrees the shadow falls east or west of the bow. Fifteen degrees equal one hour. Estimate the time.

Another quick trick is estimating the time to sunset. While holding your hand at arm's length, estimate how many horizontal fingers there are between the horizon and the sun. Each finger equals about fifteen minutes. Four fingers to sunset equals one hour; six fingers equals one and a half hours.

Starting a Fire - Another survival skill to learn is how to start a fire without matches. Matches and lighters can get wet and will no longer work. If you are on a longer trip, you should be carrying other forms of ignition. Flint and steel is probably the most popular. You can also bring a magnesium block and/or some tinder. Magnesium is good because it can get wet and it will still catch a spark. Other choices are cotton balls, dryer lint, and charred cloth. All need to be protected from moisture (film canisters work great). To make charred cloth, visit Borealfyr.com. The forest can also provide you with dry duff (vegetation), pine straw, cedar leafs, cedar bark scrapings, and birch paper.

Experiment with different materials and methods to start a fire. You may not always have the materials you are used to. After a while you will develop favorites. Mine is flint and steel over char cloth nestled in cedar bark scrapings served on birch paper.

Another method for the more ambitious sort is the fire bow drill. This is a proven way of starting a fire using only primitive tools. It is an arduous task that takes practice to master. If you are interested, go online. There are many sites that offer good tips and techniques.

Shelters - Another skill to consider is building a shelter. Obviously you are not going to do this in the Boundary Waters area unless it is a real survival situation. What you can do is explore the area around your campsite (be sure to orient yourself first). Imagine what you would do without any equipment. Look for an area that provides protection from the wind and possible rain. Consider rock overhangs, fallen (stable) trees, thick conifer boughs, caves, and even abandoned dens.

You can build quick structures by leaning branches against boulders or root beds from toppled trees. Add cedar, pine, or spruce boughs over them for wind and rain protection. Or find a stand of conifers. Lay a long branch between two lower limbs, about four feet off the ground. Build a wall of branches and boughs on the windward side. Put down branches, boughs, and leaves as bedding to keep the ground chill off of you. At night cover yourself with boughs and leaves.

Make a wikiup (teepee). Lay branches against an existing tree or lash three or four branches together at the top. Add more branches and weave saplings through for strength. You can layer in boughs and leaves for wind and rain protection.

If you still have an overwhelming urge to build something, drag a dead branch back to camp. Use it to build scale-model structures. A one-foot-equals-one-inch scale works great. Build a lean-to using Y posts. Layer the walls with twigs and cedar leaves. Test its stability and tweak your design as needed; add a second wall to make an A-frame. Build a miniature wikiup. When you are done, snap a few pictures then toss the whole mess into the fire.

Rich Annen

Chapter Nine

Trips

In this chapter, I have charted a number of trips that might interest you. They are subjective on my part. If you look to your planning maps, you can find many more that may suit your desires. I shy away from the heavily used or motor lakes, though some can't be avoided. Being towed is another luxury I avoid. A tow will get you to the interior quicker, but I think it takes away from the overall experience. The duration of these trips is an estimate. Your actual duration is dependent on your traveling abilities (paddle, portage) and how much leisure time you like.

Short Trips (1-3 days)

Loon Lake
Entry #: 14, Little Indian Sioux River   **Trailhead:** Same
Route: L.I.S.R., Upper Pauness, Lower Pauness, L.I.S.R., Loon. Return following entry route.
Sights: Cascades, bluff
Paddle miles: 18   **Portage miles:** 2
Total miles: 20   **Duration:** 2-3 days

Ensign Lake
Entry #: 25, Moose Lake.   **Trailhead:** Same
Route: Moose, Newfound, Splash, Ensign.
Return following entry route.
Paddle miles: 16   **Portage miles:** 0.3
Total miles: 16.3   **Duration:** 2-3 days

Ensign Lake
Entry #: 27, Snowbank Lake.   **Trailhead:** Same
Route: Snowbank, Boot, Ensign. Return following entry route.
Paddle miles: 11   **Portage miles:** 2
Total miles: 13   **Duration:** 2-3 days

Perent Lake
Entry #: 36, Hog Creek   **Trailhead:** Same
Route: Hog Creek, Perent Lake. Return following entry route.
Paddle miles: 4-8   **Portage miles:** 0
Total miles: 4-8   **Duration:** 2-3 days

Polly Lake
Entry #: 37, Kawishiwi Lake   **Trailhead:** Same
Route: Kawishiwi, Kawishiwi River, Square River, Kawasachong, Townline, Polly. Return following entry route.
Paddle miles: 12   **Portage miles:** 2
Total miles: 14   **Duration:** 2-3 days

Beth Lake
Entry #: 38, Sawbill   **Trailhead:** Same
Route: Sawbill, Alton, Beth. Return following entry route.
Paddle miles: 8   **Portage miles:** 1
Total miles: 9   **Duration:** 2-3 days

Grace Lake
Entry #: 38, Sawbill   **Trailhead:** Same
Route: Sawbill, Alton, Beth, Grace. Return following entry route.
Paddle miles: 11   **Portage miles:** 3
Total miles: 14   **Duration:** 2-3 days

Brule Lake
Entry #: 41, Brule **Trailhead:** Same
Route: Brule
Paddle miles: 1-6 **Portage miles:** 0
Total miles: 1-6 **Duration:** 2-3 days

Long Island Lake
Entry #: 50, Cross Bay **Trailhead:** Cross River
Route: Cross River, Ham, Cross Bay, Rib, Lower George, Karl, Long Island. Return following entry route.
Paddle miles: 14 **Portage miles:** 1.5
Total miles: 15.5 **Duration:** 2-3 days

Tuscarora Lake
Entry #: 51, Missing Link **Trailhead:** Round
Route: Round, Missing Link, Tuscarora. Return following entry route.
Paddle miles: 5 **Portage miles:** 3.5
Total miles: 8.5 **Duration:** 2-3 days

Brant Lake
Entry #: 52, Brant **Trailhead:** Round
Route: Round, West Round, Edith, Brant. Return following entry route.
Paddle miles: 4 **Portage miles:** 1
Total miles: 5 **Duration:** 2-3 days

Alpine Lake
Entry #: 54, Seagull
Trailhead: Blankenburg Landing or outfitter
Route: Seagull, Alpine. Return following entry route.
Paddle miles: 14 **Portage miles:** 0.7
Total miles: 14.7 **Duration:** 2-3 days

Rich Annen

Seagull Lake
Entry #: 54, Seagull
Trailhead: Blankenburg Landing or outfitter
Route: Seagull
Sights: Bluffs
Paddle miles: 1-10   **Portage miles:** 0
Total miles: 1-10   **Duration:** 2-3 days

Seagull, Saganaga lakes (loop)
Entry #: 54, Seagull
Trailhead: Blankenburg Landing or outfitter
Route: Seagull, Grandpa, Roy, Saganaga, Red Rock, Alpine, Seagull
Paddle miles: 19.3   **Portage miles:** 1.7
Total miles: 21   **Duration:** 2-3 days

Saganaga Lake
Entry #: 55, Saganaga
Trailhead: Sag Lake or Moose Pond landings
Routes: 2 hours (5 miles) to Horseshoe Island,
 2 hours (5 miles) to Munker or Voyageurs Islands,
 2 hours (6 miles) to Long Island,
 3 hours (8 miles) to Red Rock Bay or James Bay.
Duration: 2-3 days
Island Loop - 6 miles to Long Island, 4.5 miles to Bradley/Government/Horseshoe Islands, 5 miles to trailhead.
Paddle miles: 15.5   **Duration:** 2-3 days

Gunflint, Saganaga lakes (shuttle)
Entry #: 57, Magnetic   **Trailhead:** Gunflint
Route: Gunflint, Magnetic, clove, Granite, Granite River, Gneiss, Devil's Elbow, Maraboeuf, Granite River, Saganaga. 11 road miles to entry point.
Sights: Rapids, falls
Paddle miles: 19.3   **Portage miles:** 1.4
Total miles: 20.7   **Duration:** 2-3 days

QPP – Pickerel Lake
Entry #: QPP 12 **Trailhead:** French
Route: French, Pickerel. Return following entry route.
Paddle miles: 16 **Portage miles:** 0
Total miles: 16 **Duration:** 2-3 days

QPP – Batchewaung Lake
Entry #: QPP 21 **Trailhead:** Nym
Route: Nym, Batchewaung. Return following entry route.
Paddle miles: 6 **Portage miles:** 1
Total miles: 7 **Duration:** 2-3 days

QPP – Quetico Lake
Entry #: QPP 32 **Trailhead:** Beaverhouse
Route: Beaverhouse, Quetico. Return following entry route.
Paddle miles: 10 **Portage miles:** 1.5
Total miles: 11.5 **Duration:** 2-3 days

QPP – Saganagons Lake
Entry #: QPP 74 **Trailhead:** Saganaga (Cache Bay)
Route: Saganaga, Cache Bay, Saganagons. Return following entry route.
Paddle miles: 25 **Portage miles:** 1
Total: 26 miles **Duration:** 2-4 days

Intermediate Trips (3-7 days)

L.I.S.R., Pocket, Loon (loop)
Entry #: 14, Little Indian Sioux River **Trailhead:** Same
Route: L.I.S.R., Upper Pauness, Lower Pauness, Shell, Little Shell, Lynx, Ruby, Hustler, Oyster, Rocky, Green, Ge-be-on-e-quet, Ge-be-on-e-quet Creek, Pocket Creek, Pocket, Finger Creek, Finger, Thumb, Beartrack, Eugene, Steep, South, Section 3 Pond, Slim, Little Loon, Loon, L.I.S.R., Lower Pauness, Upper Pauness river, trailhead.
Sights: Devil's Cascade
Paddle miles: 37.3 **Portage miles:** 7.4
Total miles: 44.7 **Duration:** 5-7 days

Rich Annen

Lac La Croix
Entry #: 16, Moose River, north   **Trailhead:** Moose River
Route: Moose River, Nina Moose, Nina Moose River, Lake Agnes, Boulder River, Lac La Croix. Return following entry route.
Sights: Pictographs, rapids
Paddle miles: 30   **Portage miles:** 3
Total miles: 33   **Duration:** 4-5 days

Moose River, Crooked, Basswood, Nels (shuttle)
Entry #: 16, Moose River   **Trailhead:** Same
Route: Moose River, Nina Moose, Nina Moose River, Lake Agnes, Boulder River, Lac La Croix, Bottle, Iron, Crooked, Basswood River, Basswood, river, Sandpit, Mudro, Picket, Nels, trailhead 15 road miles from entry.
Sights: Rapids, Warrior Hill, Curtain Falls, bays, Table Rock, pictographs, Basswood Falls
Paddle miles: 46.4   **Portage miles:** 4.9
Total miles: 51.3   **Duration:** 5-7 days

South Hegman, Fourtown (loop)
Entry #: 77, S. Hegman   **Trailhead:** same
Route: South Hegman, North Hegman, Trease, Angleworm, Home, Gull, Gun, Fairy, Boot, Fourtown, bay, Horse, Tin Can, Sand Pit, Mudro, Picket, river, Nels, river, South Hegman
Sights: Pictographs
Paddle miles: 18.8   **Portage miles:** 5.3
Total miles: 24.1   **Duration:** 4-5 days

Basswood River
Entry #: 24, Fall Lake   **Trailhead:** Same
Route: Fall, Newton, Pipestone Bay, Basswood, Basswood River. Return following entry route.
Sights: Rapids, falls
Paddle miles: 20-30   **Portage miles:** 1
Total miles: 21-31   **Duration:** 3-4 days

Moose Lake, Knife (loop)
Entry #: 25, Moose Lake **Trailhead:** Moose Lake
Route: Moose, Newfound, Sucker, Birch, Carp, Melon, Seed, Portage, Knife, Vera, Ensign, Splash, Newfound, Moose.
Sights: Falls, Pine Isle (Root Beer Lady site)
Paddle miles: 38 **Portage miles:** 2
Total miles: 40 **Duration:** 3-5 days

Snowbank, Knife (loop)
Entry #: 27, Snowbank **Trailhead:** Same
Route: Snowbank, Disappointment, Ahsub, Jitterbug, Adventure, Cattyman, Jordan, Ima, Hatchet, ponds, Thomas, Fraser, Gerund, Ahmakose, Wisini, Strup, Kekekabic, ponds, Eddy, Knife, Vera, Ensign, Boot, pond, Snowbank.
Sights: Disappointment Mountain, falls, Pine Isle (Root Beer Lady site)
Paddle miles: 39.7 **Portage miles:** 4.5
Total miles: 44.2 **Duration:** 5-7 days

Lake Insula
Entry #: 30, Lake One **Trailhead:** Lake One
Route: Lake One, Lake Two, Lake Three, Lake Four, Hudson, Insula. Return following entry route.
Paddle miles: 36 **Portage miles:** 1.5
Total miles: 37.5 **Duration:** 3-5 days

Kawishiwi, river, Lake One (shuttle)
Entry #: 37, Kawishiwi Lake **Trailhead:** Same
Route: Kawishiwi, Kawishiwi River, Square, river, Kawasachong, Townline, Polly, river, Koma, Malberg, river, Alice, river, Insula, Hudson, river, Four, Three, Two, pond, One, trailhead entry point # 30. 87 road miles from entry.
Sights: Pictographs.
Paddle miles: 36.8 **Portage miles:** 3
Total miles: 39.8 **Duration:** 4-6 days

Kawishiwi, Ledge (loop)
Entry #: 37, Kawishiwi Lake   **Trailhead:** Same
Route: Kawishiwi, Kawishiwi River, Square, river, Kawasachong, Townline, Polly, river, Koma, Malberg, river, Kivania, Anit, Pan, Panhandle, pond, Makwa, Hoe, Fee, Vee, Ledge, pond, Boulder, pond, Adams, Beaver, Trapline, river, Malberg, return following entry route.
Paddle miles: 33   **Portage miles:** 7.6
Total miles: 40.6   **Duration:** 5-7 days

Phoebe
Entry #: 38, Sawbill   **Trailhead:** Same
Route: Sawbill, Alton, Beth, Grace, Grace River, Phoebe. Return following entry route.
Paddle miles: 14   **Portage miles:** 4
Total miles: 18   **Duration:** 3-5 days

Sawbill, Cherokee (loop)
Entry #: 38, Sawbill   **Trailhead:** Same
Route: Sawbill, Smoke, Burnt, Kelly, Jack, Weird, pond, South Temperance, North Temperance, Sitka, Cherokee, Cherokee Creek, Skoop, Ada, Ada Creek, Sawbill
Paddle miles: 16   **Portage miles:** 4.8
Total miles: 20.8   **Duration:** 4-5 days

Sawbill, Polly, Malberg, Zenith, (loop). Five rivers trip
Entry #: 38, Sawbill   **Trailhead:** Same
Route: Sawbill, Alton, Beth, Grace, Grace River, Phoebe, Knight, Phoebe River, Hazel, river, Polly, Kawishiwi River, Koma, Malberg, Louse River, Frond, Boze, river, Trail, river, Bug, Louse, Poe, Mug, Wine, Frederick, Zenith, Lujenida, Kelso River, Kelso, river, Sawbill.
Paddle miles: 29   **Portage miles:** 7.8
Total miles: 36.8   **Duration:** 5-6 days

Ram, Cherokee, Bower Trout. Misquah Hills (loop)
Entry #: 44, Ram **Trailhead:** Same
Route: Ram, Kroft, Rum, Little Trout, Misquah, Vista, Horseshoe, Gaskin, Winchell, Omega, Kaskadinna, Muskeg, river, Long Island, Long Island River, Gordan, Cherokee, Sitka, North Temperance, South Temperance, Brule, Vernon, Swan, pond, Skidway, Dugout, Marshall, Bower Trout. One mile from entry point.
Sights: Misquah Hills
Paddle miles: 32.9   **Portage miles:** 6.3
Total: 39.2   **Duration:** 5-6 days

Cross Bay, Frost, river, Round (loop)
Entry #: 50, Cross Bay   **Trailhead:** Cross River
Route: Cross River, Ham, Cross Bay, Rib, Lower George, Karl, Long Island, Long   Island River, Gordon, Unload, Frost, Frost River, Octopus, river, Chase, Pencil, river, Afton, Fente, Whipped, Mora, Tarry, Crooked, Gillis, Bat, Green, Flying, Gotter, Brant, Edith, West Round, Round. 0.3 road miles from entry.
Sights: Rapids
Paddle miles: 26.1   **Portage miles:** 4.9
Total miles: 31   **Duration:** 5-6 days

Crooked (loop)
Entry #: 51, Missing Link   **Trailhead:** Round
Route: Round, Missing Link, Tuscarora, Owl, Crooked, Gillis, Bat, Green, Flying, Gotter, Brant, Edith, West Round, Round.
Paddle miles: 11   **Portage miles:** 4
Total miles: 15   **Duration:** 3-4 days

Round, Little Saganaga.
The Land of Sky Blue Waters (loop)
Entry #: 51, Missing Link **Trailhead:** Round
Route: Round, Missing Link, Tuscarora, Owl, Crooked, Tarry, Mora, Little Saganaga, Virgin, West Fern, Powell, French, Seahorse, Warclub, Fay, Flying, Gotter, Brant, Edith, West Round, Round.
Sights: Purported site of the famous Hamm's Beer photo, Little Saganaga Lake (48° 1.926 N x 90° 59.268 W) looking north.
Paddle miles: 21 **Portage miles:** 5
Total miles: 26 **Duration:** 4-5 days

Round, Knife, Saganaga (shuttle)
Entry #: 52, Brant **Trailhead:** Round
Route: Round, West Round, Edith, Brant, Gotter, Flying, Fay, Warclub, Seahorse, French, Peter, Gabimichigami, Agamok, Mueller, Ogishkemuncie, Annie, Jenny, Eddy, Knife, Ottertrack, Swamp, Saganaga. Nine road miles from entry.
Sights: Falls, Pine Isle (Root Beer Lady site), Monument Portage
Paddle miles: 44 **Portage miles:** 3
Total miles: 47 **Duration:** 5-7 days

Ogishkemuncie
Entry #: 54, Seagull **Trailhead:** Same
Route: Seagull, Alpine, Jasper, Kingfisher, Ogishkemuncie. Return following entry route.
Paddle miles: 28 **Portage miles:** 1.3
Total miles: 29.3 **Duration:** 3-4 days

Extended Trips (6-plus days)

Voyageurs Route, Crane to McFarland (shuttle)
Entry #: 12, Little Vermilion   **Trailhead:** Crane
Route: Crane, Sand Point, Little Vermilion, Loon River, Loon, Lac La Croix, Bottle, Iron, Crooked, Basswood River, Basswood, Sucker, Birch, Melon, Seed, Knife, Ottertrack, Swamp, Saganaga, Maraboeuf, Devil's Elbow, Gneiss, Granite River, Granite Bay, Granite, Clove, Pine River, Magnetic, Gunflint, Little Gunflint, Little North, North, South, Rat, Rose, Rove, Watap, Mountain, Fan, Vaseux, Moose, North Fowl, Royal, Royal River, John, Little John, Trailhead (McFarland). 235 road miles from entry point.
Sights: Narrows, Falls, Rapids, Warrior Hill, Table Rock, Falls, Laurentian Divide
Paddle miles: 172   **Portage miles:** 9
Total miles: 181   **Duration:** 15-17 days

*L.I.S.R. to Saganaga (shuttle), Sigurd Olson Route**
Entry #: 14, L.I.S.R, north   **Trailhead:** Same
Route: L.I.S.R., Upper Pauness, Lower Pauness, river, Loon, Lac La Croix, Bottle, Iron, Crooked, Basswood River, Basswood, Prairie Portage RS, Sucker, Birch, Carp, Melon, Seed, Knife, Ottertrack, Swamp, Saganaga. 192 road miles from entry.
Sights: Devils Cascade, pictographs, rapids, falls, Warrior Hill, Table Rock
Paddle miles: 135   **Portage miles:** 5.1
Total miles: 140.1   **Duration:** 10-12 days
*Route taken from Olson's book, *The Singing Wilderness*, Part Two, Chapter 4, "Farewell to Saganaga."

Rich Annen

Baker, Frost River (loop)
Entry #: 39, Baker **Trailhead:** Same
Route: Baker, Peterson, Kelly, Jack, Weird, Temperance River, South Temperance, North Temperance, Sitka, Cherokee, Gordon, Unload, Frost, Frost River, Chase, Pencil, river, Afton, Fente, Hub, Mesaba, Hug, Duck, Zenith, Lujenida, Kelso River, Kelso, river, Sawbill, Smoke, Burnt, Kelly, Peterson, Baker.
Sights: Rapids
Paddle miles: 31 **Portage miles:** 9
Total miles: 40 **Duration:** 6-8 days

Round, Kekekabic, Seagull (shuttle)
Entry #: 51, Missing Link **Trailhead:** Round
Route: Round, Missing Link, Tuscarora, Owl, Crooked, Tarry, Mora, Little Saganaga, pond, Elton, Makwa, pond, Panhandle, Pan, Anit, Kivaniva, Kiwishiwi River, pond, Alice, Insula, Recline, Kiana, Thomas, Fraser, Gerund, Ahmakose, Wisini, Strup, Kekekabic, ponds, Eddy, Jenny, Annie, Ogishkemuncie, Kingfisher, Alpine, Rog, Seagull. Seven road miles to entry.
Paddle miles: 52 **Portage miles:** 6.4
Total miles: 58.4 **Duration:** 6-8 days

QPP – Beaverhouse: Sturgeon Lake (loop)
Entry #: 32, Beaverhouse
Trailhead: Beaverhouse Ranger Station
Route: Beaverhouse, Quetico, Badwater, Fair, Your, Snow, Trail, Bent Pine Creek, Sturgeon, Lonely, Yeh, Little Jean, Jean, Conk, Quetico, Beaverhouse.
Paddle miles: 60 **Portage miles:** 5
Total miles: 65 **Duration:** 6-8 days

QPP - Prairie Portage: Kahshahpiwi, Sturgeon, Maligne River (loop)
Entry #: BWCAW 25, Moose Lake; QPP 53, Kahshahpiwi.
Trailhead: Moose Lake
Route: Moose, Newfound, Sucker, Prairie Portage RS, Bayley Bay, Burke, North Bay, Isabella, Dell, Grey, Yum Yum, Kahshahpiwi, Keefer, Sark, Cairn, river, Shelley, Keats, Chatterton, Russell, Sturgeon, Maligne River, Tanner, river, Minn, river, Darky, Brent, McIntyre, Sarah, Side, Isabella. Return following entry route.
Sights: Pictographs, rapids, falls
Paddle miles: 115 **Portage miles:** 7+
Total miles: 122+ **Duration:** 11-13 days

QPP - Prairie Portage: Agnes, Kawnipi, Falls, Man Chain, Birch (loop)
Entry #: BWCAW 25, Moose Lake. QPP 61, Agnes Lake
Trailhead: Moose Lake
Route: Moose, Newfound, Sucker, Prairie Portage RS, Basswood, Sunday, Meadows, Agnes, unknown, Keewatin, Kawnipi, Kenny, river, Saganagons, Slate, Fran, Bell, Bit, unknown, Other Man, This Man, unknown, That Man, Sheridan, Carp, Birch, Sucker, Newfound, Moose.
Sights: Pictographs, falls
Paddle miles: 78 **Portage miles:** 5
Total miles: 83 **Duration:** 8-9 days

QPP - Cache Bay: Saganaga, Man Lakes Chain (loop)
Entry #: BWCAW 55, Saganaga. QPP 72, Man Lakes Chain
Trailhead: Saganaga
Route: Saganaga (tow to American Point?), Cache Bay RS, Saganagons, Slate, Fran, unnamed, Bell, unnamed, unnamed, Other Man, This Man, No Man, That Man, Sheridan, Carp, Emerald, Plough, Ottertrack, Swamp, Saganaga.
Paddle miles: 53.5 **Portage miles:** 3.8
Total miles: 57.3 **Duration:** 5-7 days

QPP - Cache Bay: Saganaga, Falls Chain, Kawnipi (loop)
Entry #: BWCAW 55, Saganaga. QPP 73, Falls Chain.
Trailhead: Saganaga
Route: Saganaga, Cache Bay RS, Saganagons, Kawnipi River, Sidney, river, Kenny, river, Kawnipi, return following entry route.
Sights: Rapids, falls
Paddle miles: 47   **Portage miles:** 3.5
Total miles: 50.5   **Duration:** 5-7 days

Chapter Ten

While You're in the Area

This area is best known for the Boundary Waters, but there are plenty of other reasons to visit. You can visit many historic sites, museums, lighthouses, waterfalls, palisades, or tour some iron mines. You can enjoy fishing, camping, hiking, biking, or kayaking and canoeing outside the Boundary Waters. Or you can choose to take a more leisurely pace and enjoy the shopping, entertainment, and dining the areas offer. Plan to spend a few days before or after your wilderness trip to visit some of these sights. Or you can plan a separate vacation to the area.

Duluth
There is a good chance that your drive will be through or near the Duluth area. Duluth/Superior offers many attractions.
- Take a drive along the West Skyline Parkway and hike to the top of the tower at Enger Park for magnificent views of the Duluth/Superior Harbors and Lake Superior.
- Visit the Canal District for shopping, entertainment, and dining. Don't forget to visit the Lake Superior Maritime Visitor

Center *(lsmma.com)* and watch the Aerial Lift Bridge in operation.
- While you are still in the harbor area stop at the Great Lakes Aquarium *(glaquarium.org)* or tour the ore carrier SS William A. Irvin *(decc.org)* or the whaleback ship the SS Meteor *(superiorpublicmuseums.org)*.

Duluth aerial lift bridge

- Stop by the Bong Veterans Historical Center *(superiorpublicmuseums.org)*.
- Visit the Lake Superior Railroad Museum *(lsrm.org)* or take a ride on the North Shore *(northshorescenicrailroad.org)* or Lake Superior & Mississippi *(lsmrr.org)* railroads.
- Visit one of the historic mansions, the Glensheen *(glensheen.org)* or the Fairlawn *(superiorpublicmuseums.org)*.

Go to ***visitduluth.com*** for a more complete listing of attractions, cost, and hours of operation.

Iron Range

If you are headed for the west side of the Boundary Waters area, you will drive up U.S. 53, which will take you through the Mesabi Iron Range. Iron mining in this area goes back more than 100 years. You can tour some of these mines and visit the museums to get an idea of the history of this region. Take U.S. 169 south to get to Chisholm and Hibbing.

Iron Man statue

- United States Hockey Hall of Fame *(ushockeyhall.com)* (Eveleth)
- Iron Man Statue (Chisholm)

- Minnesota Discovery Center (*mndiscoverycenter.com*). (Chisholm).
- Minnesota Museum of Mining (*mnmuseumofmining.org*). (Chisholm).
- Hull-Rust-Mahoning Mine overlook. (Hibbing).
- Greyhound Bus Museum (*greyhoundbusmuseum.org*). (Hibbing).
- Drive past Bob Dylan's childhood home (a private home not open to the public). (Hibbing).

Go to ***irontrail.org*** for more attractions and to help plan your visit.

Back to U.S. 53 and north to Cook. Visit the La Croix Ranger Station and get a copy of the *Discovery Auto Tour* ($3.00). It offers two auto tours of the west side of the Superior National Forest. The tour offers numbered stops that correspond with the descriptions in the book. The first, Vermilion Falls Tour, takes you north on County Highway 24 through Buyck to Crane Lake. After a stop at Vermilion Falls you head back through Cusson and Orr to Cook. Allow four to five hours for this tour.

The Voyageur

The second, Echo Trail Tour, also takes you north on County Highway 24 but then turns east on the Echo Trail, County Highway 116. You will follow the Echo Trail to Ely. The lower third of this trail is probably the closest you will ever get to nature while seated in a car. From Ely you follow State Highway 1 west through Soudan and Tower and back to Cook. Allow six to seven hours for this tour. You can start and end either of these tours anywhere along the way.

From Cook, you can continue north on U.S. Highway 53 to Voyageurs National Park. Voyageurs National Park offers camping at designated sites throughout the Park. These sites are only accessible by boat. You can canoe, motorboat, or rent a houseboat. Reservations are required so, to plan your trip, go online to *nps.gov/Voyageurs*.

Ely

Most of us will turn on State Highway 169 north near Virginia and head toward Ely. Along the way you will pass Lake Vermilion. The lake offers camping, fishing, and numerous resorts. As you pass near Tower, visit the Bois Forte Heritage Center to see the history of the Ojibwe in this area. Or stop at the Tower-Soudan Historical Society Historical Center located in a historic train depot (*lakevermilionchamber.com*).

As you continue north on State Highway 169, you will come to Soudan. Soudan is home to the Soudan Underground Mine State Park. This is a "do not miss" in my book. Where else can you go on a tour 2,341 feet underground? (*dnr.state.mn.us/Soudan Underground Mine*).

Pioneer Mine

Continuing north on State Highway 169, you will arrive at Ely. Ely is the hub for this area and, as such, it has many attractions. Camping, fishing, hiking, biking, skiing, snowshoeing and dog sledding (in season) are all possibilities. Or you can enjoy the shopping, entertainment, and dining opportunities.

- *International Wolf Center* – Exhibits and information on wolves and their interaction with man. You also have a chance to observe the resident wolf pack (*wolf.org*).

Kawishiwi Falls

- ***North American Bear Center*** – Exhibits and demonstrations pertaining to all bears of North America. Viewing area of resident bears in a two-acre enclosure *(bear.org)*.
- ***Dorothy Molter Museum*** – The last resident of the Boundary Waters. She was known as the "Root Beer Lady" because she would make and sell root beer to passing canoeists. After her death in 1986, two of her cabins were relocated to this site *(rootbeerlady.com)*.
- ***Ely Arts & Heritage Center*** – Located at the Pioneer Mine on Pioneer Road. The Heritage Center is open in the summer on Tuesdays and Fridays from 1 to 4 p.m. At other hours, the buildings and headframe are visible along with an overlook of Miners Lake. Miners Lake is a result of the natural flooding of the five mines that were operated at this site until 1967 *(elygreenstone.org)*.
- ***Ely-Winton History Museum*** – Located at the Vermilion Community College. Open weekdays 10 a.m. to 4 p.m.

- ***Kawishiwi Falls*** - Five miles east of town off the Fernberg Road, State Highway 169. Look for the signs. A three-quarter-mile trail (one-and-a-half miles round trip) takes you to this seventy-foot falls between Garden and Fall Lakes.

For a more complete listing of area attractions, go to ***ely.org***.

North Shore

If you are headed to the Sawbill or the Gunflint, you will be driving on scenic State Highway 61. This road is a vacation in itself. As you drive along the shore of Lake Superior, you will pass numerous waterfalls, state parks, lighthouses, and museums.

- ***Two Harbors*** – Visit the historic waterfront and see the ore docks, lighthouse, and the Lake County Historical Museum (*twoharbors.com*).
- ***Gooseberry Falls State Park*** – Three-tiered waterfalls dropping a total of ninety feet. Modern visitor center. Easy trails to all falls. The area below the falls is barrier-free so you can go out on the river rock to get that perfect picture (*dnr.state.mn.us/State Parks/Gooseberry Falls*).
- ***Split Rock Lighthouse and Historic Site*** – Tour the lighthouse, keepers' houses, and out buildings of this 1910 light station (*splitrocklighthouse.org*).
- ***Palisade Head*** – Scenic overlook of Lake Superior. Parking off of Highway 61. A narrow road leads from the parking lot to the top of the palisade.

Split Rock Lighthouse

- ***Tettegouche State Park*** – Visit the seventy-foot Baptism River falls. It is one of the tallest in the state. Take a hike out to Shovel Point for a 170-foot-high overlook of Lake Superior *(dnr.state.mn.us/ State Parks/ Tettegouche)*.

Baptism Falls

- ***Temperance River State Park*** – It's an easy pullover and a short walk to the falls. Great viewing areas of cascades and falls. Be sure to visit both the upper and lower gorges *(dnr.state.mn.us/State Parks/ Temperance River)*.
- **Tofte Ranger Station** – If you are headed to the Sawbill area of the Boundary Waters, this is where you can pick up your permit, or get forest information on sights, camping, hiking, biking, and forest conditions *(fs.fed.us/superior)*.
- **Lutsen Mountain** – Take a ride on the aerial tramway to the top of Moose Mountain while crossing the cascading Poplar River. Or get your thrills on the Alpine Slide. Views of the surrounding Sawtooth Mountains and Lake Superior *(lutsen.com/Sawtooth Mountain Park)*.
- **Eagle Mountain** – From Lutsen take the Caribou Trail, County Highway 4, north. Turn east on Forest Road 170, The Grade, to the trailhead. A two-and-a-half-mile hike (five miles round trip) gets you to the top of the tallest point in Minnesota.

- *Cascade River State Park* – An easy pullover and a short walk gets you views of the river cascading through the river gorge *(dnr.state.mn.us/State Parks/Cascade River)*.
- *Grand Marais* – Best chance to stock up on supplies and visit:
  o The old Gunflint Trail sign on 2nd Avenue West.
  o Walk out on Artist Point.
  o Stop at the World's Best Donuts for a sweet treat.
- *Judge C. R. Magney State Park* – Visit the mysterious Devil's Kettle Falls. Use the parking lot inside the park. A one-mile hike will get you to the falls *(dnr.state.mn.us/State Parks/Judge C. R. Magney)*. There is a fee.
- *Grand Portage National Monument* – Visit the Heritage Center and the Historic Depot or hike parts or the entire 8.7-mile (17.4 miles round trip) Grand Portage footpath to Fort Charlotte on the Pigeon River *(nps.gov/grpo)*.
- *Grand Portage State Park* - A half-mile hike will get you to great viewing areas of the 100-foot High Falls of the Pigeon River, 1.5 miles to Middle Falls. These falls along with other rapids and falls further up river was the reason that the grand portage had to be established *(dnr.state.mn.us/State Parks/Grand Portage)*.

If you wish, continue to enjoy the sights of Superior's north shore in Canada or you can drive around the entire lake. But that is another vacation.

For more complete information on touring the north shore, go to **northshorevisitor.com**.

Gunflint Trail

County Highway 12 north out of Grand Marais is the historic Gunflint Trail. This trail is surrounded by the Superior National Forest and offers many recreational opportunities. There are many lodges and outfitters to assist you in your pursuit. Fuel up before you leave Grand Marais as there are no cheap gas stations on the Trail. Some businesses do sell gas but at a steep price.

An old postcard

- ***Old Gunflint Trail Entrance*** – Check out the old entrance sign to the Gunflint. Located on 2nd Avenue West, just north of Highway 61, across from the Dairy Queen.
- ***Gunflint Ranger Station*** – Before you leave town, stop at the Ranger Station to pick up your Boundary Waters permit. Or get forest information on sights, camping, hiking, biking, and forest conditions *(fs.fed.us/superior)*.
- ***Pincushion Mountain Overlook*** – Enjoy a panoramic view of Grand Marais and Lake Superior.
- ***Clearwater Lodge*** – Historic lodge founded in 1915. The main log lodge was built in 1926 and is still in use. Be sure to stop at the bakery (clearwaterhistoriclodge.com).
- ***Trail Center*** – Stop for a beer and a bite to eat. Pick up last-minute supplies. Check out the selection of homemade dehydrated meals (trailcenterlodge.com).
- ***Old Gunflint Trail*** – Iron Lake Road, County Highway 92, takes you down four-and-a-half miles of the original road grade.

- ***Centennial Trail*** – Take a hike along a 3.3-mile looped trail and visit the site of the short-lived Paulsen Mine (1893-1894). The north portion of the trail follows the Kekekabic Trail while the south portion follows the old railroad bed. *(fs.fed.us/superior, follow hiking links).*
- ***Magnetic Rock*** – Take a 1.5-mile hike (three miles round trip) and visit Magnetic Rock, a thirty-foot monolith. The 2007 Ham Lake Fire made the rock more visible. Bring a compass along to test the magnetic attraction of the rock. *(fs.fed.us/superior, follow hiking links).*
- ***Chic-Wauk Museum*** – At the end of the Trail on Moose Pond Drive. Visit this old lodge that was converted to an historic museum of the Trail and its people *(chikwauk.com).*

For more complete information on touring the Gunflint, go to ***fs.fed.us/superior*** *or **visitcookcounty.com***

Appendix 1

First Aid Kit

Item and Use

Dressings

12	1" Band-Aids	Cover cuts, blisters, burns
4	2x2 gauze pads	Cover cuts, blisters, burns
2	4x4 gauze pads	Cover cuts, burns
2	5x9 gauze pads	Cover cuts, burns
4	Butterflies	Wound closure

Bandaging

1	1" Kling	Secure dressings
1	3" Kling	Secure dressings
1	4" elastic wrap	Support strains/sprains
1 roll	1" athletic (hockey) tape	Secure dressings, support strains/sprains

See more on next page.

Cleansing
12	Antiseptic towelettes	Clean wounds
1	Antiseptic soap	Clean wounds
1	Sterile water/saline	Flush wounds
1	10 ml syringe (for flush)	Flush foreign objects from eyes
6	Cotton swabs (Q-Tips)	Clean wounds, remove foreign objects from eyes/ears

Ointments
1	Antibiotic cream	Wound care

Medications
50	Advil/ibuprofen	Pain, inflammation
20	Tums/antacid	Indigestion
20	Pepto Bismol	Abdominal pain, nausea, diarrhea
12	Benadryl	Allergies, bug bites

Miscellaneous
1 tweezers	Slivers/tick removal	
4 pair	Non-latex sterile gloves	Wound protection
1 scissors	Cut dressings/bandages/tape	Cut away dead tissue from blisters

In addition, you should also carry:
1 tb	sunblock	Skin protection
1 btl	Aloe with Lidocaine lotion	Sun burn, bug bites
1 roll	Duct tape	Blister protection, secure dressings, support strains/sprains, immobilization

Appendix 2

Boundary Waters Canoe Area Entry Points

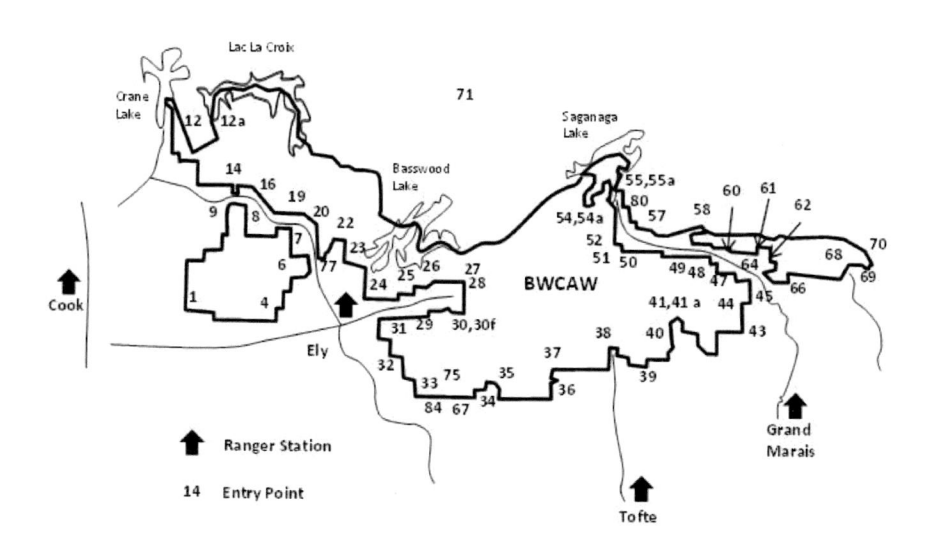

See entry point names and daily permit figures on next pages.

Entry Point and Daily Permits

1	Trout Lake	14
4	Crab Lake	4
6	Slim Lake	2
7	From Big Lake	2
8	Moose River, south	1
9	Little Indian Sioux River	1
12	Little Vermilion Lake	6
12a	Lac La Croix	8
14	L.I.S.R., north	6
16	Moose/Portage River, north	7
19	Stuart River	1
20	Angleworm Lake	2
22	Mudro Lake, restricted	2
23	Mudro Lake	6
24	Fall Lake	14
25	Moose Lake	27
26	Wood Lake	2
27	Snowbank Lake	8
28	Snowbank Lake, only	1
29	North Kawishiwi River	1
30	Lake One	7
30f	Lake One, restricted	7
31	Farm Lake	3
32	South Kawishiwi River	2
33	Little Gabbro Lake	2
34	Island River	1
35	Isabella Lake	2
36	Hog Creek	5
37	Kawishiwi Lake	9
38	Sawbill Lake	14
39	Baker Lake	3
40	Homer Lake	2
41	Brule Lake	7

Entry Point and Daily Permits

42	Brule Lake, only	3
43	Bower Trout Lake	1
44	Ram Lake	1
45	Morgan Lake south	1
47	Lizz and Swamp, lakes	4
48	Meeds Lake	3
49	Skipper and Portage lakes	2
50	Cross Bay Lake	3
51	Missing Link Lake	5
52	Brant Lake	4
54	Seagull Lake	11
54a	Seagull Lake, only	2
55	Saganaga Lake	17
55a	Saganaga, only	3
57	Magnetic Lake	3
58	South Lake	3
60	Duncan Lake	3
61	Daniels Lake	1
62	Clearwater Lake	3
64	East Bearskin Lake	4
66	Crocodile River	1
67	Bog Lake	1
68	Pine Lake	1
69	John Lake	1
70	North Fowl Lake	2
71	Trips from Canada	3
75	Little Isabella River	1
77	South Hegman	2
80	Larch Creek	1
84	Snake River	1

Data from the U.S. Forest Service, accurate as of 2015.

Rich Annen

Appendix 3

Quetico Provincial Park

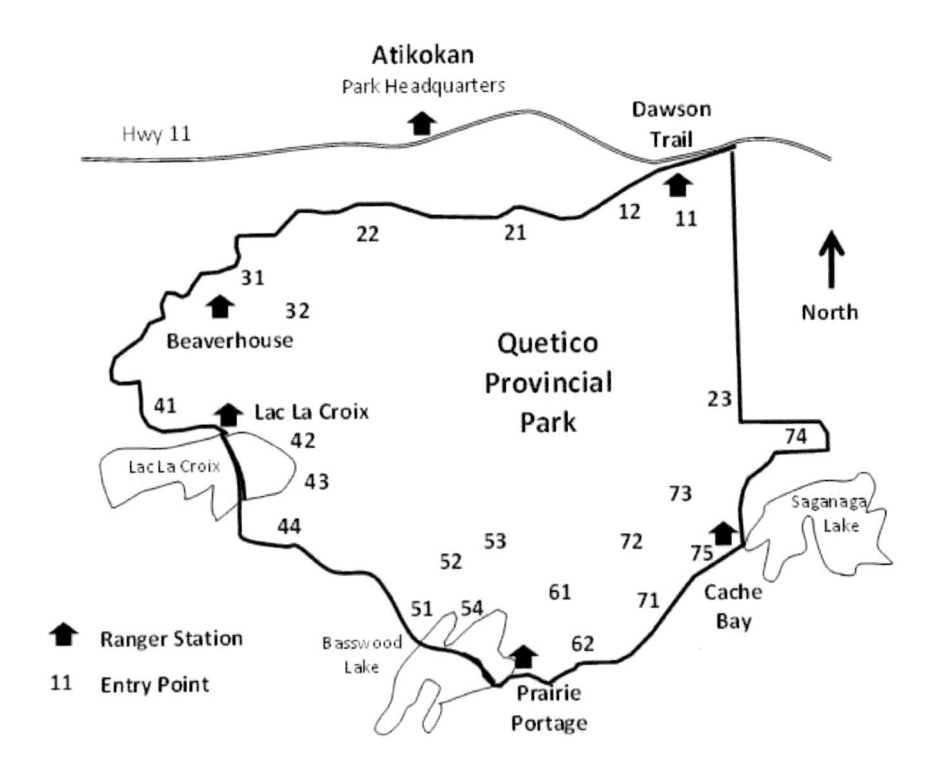

Entry Points
Daily Permit Quotas

Ranger Station	Entry Point	Daily Permits	Resident	Non-Res.
North				
Dawson Trail	11-Baptism Creek	2	2	1
	12-Pickerel Lake	10	10	3
Atikokan	21-Batchewaung Lk.	7	7	2
	22-Sue Falls	3	3	1
	23-Mac Lake	3	3	3
Beaverhouse Lake	31-Cirrus Lake	2	2	1
	32-Quetico Lake	6	6	3
West				
Lac La Croix	41-Three Mile Lake	2	2	2
	42-Maligne River	2	2	2
	43-McAree Lake	2	2	2
	44-Bottle River	2	2	1
South				
Prairie Portage	51-Basswood River	2	2	2
	52-Sarah Lake	2	2	2
	53-Kahshahpiwi Lk.	2	2	2
	54-Kings Point (fly in)	2	2	1
	61-Agnes Lake	7	7	7
	62-Carp Lake	2	2	2
Southeast				
Cache Bay	71-Knife Lake	2	2	2
	72-Man Lakes Chain	2	2	2
	73-Falls Chain	3	3	3
	74-Boundary Point, Saganagons Lake	2	2	2
	75-Cache Bay (fly in) Saganaga Lake	1	1	0

Note:
Nonresidents can qualify as a resident if they book through a Canadian outfitter or if they call no more than four days before their entry date. *Data from Ontario Parks, accurate as of 2015.*

Appendix 4

Outfitters

The following is a partial list of outfitters. Most will be able to reserve and issue your Boundary Waters permits. Visit their websites or call to get a listing of their services.

Crane Lake Area

Anderson Canoe Outfitters
7255 Crane Lake Rd.
Crane Lake, MN 55725
anderson-outfitters.com
800-777-7186

Ely Area

Boundary Waters Guide Service
529 E. Sheridan St.
Ely, MN 55731
boundarywatersguideservice.com
218-343-7951

Boundary Waters Outfitters
629 Kawishiwi Tr.
Ely, MN 55731
boundarywatersoutfitters.com
218-365-3466   800-777-8574

Canadian Border Outfitters
14635 Canadian Border Rd.
Ely, MN 55731
canoetrip.com
800-247-7530

Canadian Waters
111 E. Sheridan St.
Ely, MN 55731
canadianwaters.com
218-365-3202   800-255-2922

Canoe Country Outfitters
629 E. Sheridan St.
Ely, MN 55731
canoecountryoutfitters.com
218-365-4046   800-752-2306

Cliff Wold's Canoe Trip Outfitting
1731 E. Sheridan St.
Ely, MN 55731
cliffwolds.com
218-365-3267   800-777-8546

Duane's Canoe Outfitters
3145 Hwy 21
Babbitt, MN 55706
explorebwcaw.com
218-827-2710   800-729-2710

Echo Trail Outfitters
3788 Fenske Lake Rd.
Ely, MN 55731
echotrailoutfitters.com
218-365-5481   877-365-5481

Ely Outdoors Company
528 E. Sheridan St.
Ely, MN 55731
paddlethebwca.com
218-365-4844

Ely Outfitting Company
529 E. Sheridan St.
Ely, MN 55731
elyoutfittingcompany.com
218-343-7951

Jasper Creek Guide Service
112 W. Sheridan St.
Ely, MN 55731
jaspercompany.com
218-365-3239

Jordan's Wilderness Shop and Outfitters
1701 Hwy 1
Ely, MN 55731
jordansoutfitters.com
800-644-9955

Kawishiwi Lodge and Outfitters
3187 Fernberg Rd.
Ely, MN 55731
lakeonecanoes.com
218-365-5487

LaTourell's
14793 Moose Lake Rd.
Ely, MN 55731
latourells.com
218-365-4531   800-365-4531

Lodge of Whispering Pines
3060 Echo Trail
Ely, MN 55731
lodgeofwhisperingpines.com
218-343-7714   800-510-2947

Moose Track Adventures
593 Kawishiwi Trail
Ely, MN 55731
moosetrackadventures.com
218-365-4106

North Country Canoe Outfitters
474 Kawishiwi Trail
Ely, MN 55731
boundarywaters.com
218-365-5581   800-552-5581

Packsack Canoe Trips and Cabins
PO Box 780
Ely, MN 55731
packsackcanoetrips.com
218-365-3788   800-365-3788

Piragis Northwoods
105 N Central Ave.
Ely, MN 55731
piragis.com
218-365-6745   800-223-6565

River Point Resort and Outfitting
12007 River Point Rd.
Ely, MN 55731
riverpointresort.com
218-365-6604   800-456-5580

Spirit of the Wilderness Outfitters
2030 E. Sheridan St.
Ely, MN 55731
elycanoetrips.com
218-365-3149   800-950-2709

Voyageur North Canoe Outfitters
1829 E. Sheridan St.
Ely, MN 55731
vnorth.com
218-365-3251   800-848-5530

Way to Go Canoe Outfitters
1557 Esterberg Rd.
Ely, MN 55731
waytogooutfitters.com
218-365-4726   218-349-0906

Wilderness Outfitters
1 E. Camp St.
Ely, MN 55731
wildernessoutfitters.com
218-365-3211   800-777-8572

Williams and Hall Wilderness Guide
14694 Vosburgh Rd.
Ely, MN 55731
williamsandhall.com
218-365-5837   800-322-5837

<u>**Gunflint Trail Area**</u>

Bearskin Wilderness Outfitters
124 E. Bearskin Rd.
Grand Marais, MN 55604
bearskinoutfitters.com
218-388-2292   800-338-4170

Bear Track Outfitting Company
2011 W. Hwy 61
Grand Marais, MN 55604
bear-track.com
218-387-1162   800-795-8068

Clearwater Canoe Outfitters & Lodge
774 Clearwater Rd.
Grand Marais, MN 55604
clearwaterhistoriclodge.com
218-388-2254   800-527-0554

Gunflint Northwoods Outfitters
143 S. Gunflint Lake Rd.
Grand Marais, MN 55604
gunflintoutfitters.com
218-388-2296   888-226-6346

Hungary Jack Outfitters
318 S. Hungary Jack Rd.
Grand Marais, MN 55604
hjo.com
218-388-2275   800-648-2922

Nor'Wester Lodge
7778 Gunflint Trail
Grand Marais, MN 55604
norwesterlodge.com
218-388-2252   800-992-4386

Rockwood Lodge & Outfitter
50 Rockwood Rd.
Grand Marais, MN 55604
rockwoodbwca.com
218-388-2242

Seagull Canoe Outfitters
12208 Gunflint Trail
Grand Marais, MN 55604
seagulloutfitters.com
218-388-2216

Tuscarora Canoe Outfitters
193 Round Lake Rd.
Grand Marais, MN 55604
tuscaroracanoe.com
218-388-2221   800-544-3843

Voyageur Canoe Outfitters
189 Sag Lake Rd.
Grand Marais, MN 55604
canoeit.com
218-388-2224   888-226-6348

Sawbill Area

Sawbill Canoe Outfitters
4620 Sawbill Trail
Tofte, MN 55615
sawbill.com
218-663-7150

Sawtooth Outfitters
7213 Hwy 61
Tofte, MN 55615
sawtoothoutfitters
218-663-7643

Canada

Canoe Canada Outfitters
300 O'Brien St.
Atikokan, Ont P0T 1C0
canoecountry.com
807-597-6418

Queti Quest
PO Box 1060
Atikokan, Ont P0T 1C0
quetiquest.com
807-929-2266

Voyageur Wilderness Program
PO Box 850
Atikokan, Ont P0T 1C0
vwp.com
807-597-2450

Wyteki Outfitters
PO Box 546
Atikokan, Ont P0T 1C0
quetico-canoe-trips.com
807-947-2391

Appendix 5

Clothing

Warm Weather

Daytime/Travel Clothing

Base-layer options
- Swimsuit **or** underwear
- T-shirt (cotton or polyester)

Second layer options
- Shorts, long pants, **or** trail pants (light cotton, wool, or nylon; zip-off legs)
- Long-sleeve T-shirt (cotton or polyester)

Top-layer options
- Rain coat and rain pants **or** water/wind-proof hooded jacket

Footwear
- Socks (cotton, wool)
- Water shoes with treaded sole, **or** old tennis shoes, **or** knee high rubber boots, **or** waterproof hiking boots

Headwear
- Wide-brim hat **or** baseball style cap.

Miscellaneous
- Sunglasses
- Bandanna
- Gloves (fingerless, leather-reinforced palm with nylon back)

Typical warm weather day

Start with a swimsuit and T-shirt under convertible trail pants (zip-off leggings) and a long-sleeve T-shirt. Add cotton socks, water shoes and a baseball cap. As the day warms up, drop the long-sleeve T-shirt and zip off your leggings. Or drop your pants and go it in your swimsuit.

Nighttime/Camp Clothing

Base layer options
- Underwear
- Long-sleeve T-shirt (cotton or polyester)

Second layer options
- Jeans, **or** trail pants, **or** military BDUs (Battle Dress Uniform, military-issued heavy-duty pants and shirt), **or** sweat pants
- Long-sleeve heavy shirt **or** long-sleeve pullover (cotton, wool, fleece) **or** sweat shirt **or** hooded sweat shirt

Top-layer options
- Rain coat and rain pants **or** water/wind-proof hooded jacket

Footwear
- Socks (cotton, wool)
- Tennis shoes, **or** boots, **or** sandals, **or** Crocs, **or** moccasins

Headwear
- Wide-brim hat, **or** baseball style cap, **or** stocking cap

Typical warm weather night

Start with long pants and a long-sleeve T-shirt. Add dry socks and warm shoes. Throw on a heavy shirt, pullover, or sweatshirt as the night cools off.

Cool Weather

Daytime/Travel Clothing

Base-layer options
- Swimsuit or underwear
- Long-sleeve T-shirt (cotton or polyester)

Second layer options
- Long pants or trail pants (light cotton, wool, or nylon)
- Long-sleeve heavy shirt **or** long sleeve pullover (cotton, wool, fleece) **or s**weat shirt **or** hooded sweat shirt

Top-layer options
- Rain coat and rain pants **or** water/wind-proof hooded jacket

Footwear
- Socks (cotton, wool)
- Water shoes with treaded sole, **or** old tennis shoes, **or** knee high rubber boots, **or** waterproofed hiking boots

Headwear
- Wide-brim hat, baseball style cap, or stocking cap

Miscellaneous
- Sunglasses
- Bandanna
- Gloves (leather-reinforced palm with nylon back)

Typical cool weather day

Start with a swimsuit and long-sleeve T-shirt under long pants (light cotton, wool, or nylon) and long-sleeve heavy shirt or pullover (cotton, wool, or fleece). Add cotton or wool socks, water shoes and a stocking hat. As the day warms up, remove the long-sleeve shirt and swap stocking hat with a baseball hat.

Nighttime/Camp Clothing

Base-layer options
- Long underwear, top and bottom (cotton, cotton blend, polyester)

Second layer options
- Jeans, **or** trail pants, **or** military BDUs, **or** sweat pants
- Long-sleeve heavy shirt **or** long-sleeve pullover (cotton, wool, fleece).

Top layer options
- Sweat shirt **or** hooded sweat shirt
- Rain coat and rain pants **or** water/wind-proof hooded jacket
- Sleeping bag

Footwear
- Socks (cotton, wool)
- Tennis shoes **or** hiking boots

Headwear
- Wide-brim hat, baseball style cap, **or** stocking cap

Typical cool weather night

Start with long underwear top and bottom. Add jeans or trail pants and a long-sleeve heavy shirt or pullover (cotton, wool, or fleece). Finish with wool socks, warm shoes, and a stocking hat. Add your rain coat or a hooded jacket on the real chilly nights.

Notes:
- Light-weight, quick-dry pants are nice for day travel.
- Your swimsuit can be used as underwear.
- The zip-off legs on your quick-dry pants convert them to shorts.
- The type of T-shirts will be dependent on the temperature.
- A warm shirt, sweatshirt or jacket is a must no matter what season. Rain gear can be used as a windbreaker.
- Your daytime socks and footwear will be wet. You will need dry pairs at night.
- Bring enough dry socks and underwear to last the duration of the trip.

Appendix 6

Camp Gear

Checklist
____Tent(s)
____Stove
____Water purifier
____Compass
____Duct tape
____50' ¼" cord
____Camp knife/axe
____Matches/lighter/flint & steel
____Boy Scout water/fire sticks
____Repair kit (needle/thread, tent patch, vinyl patch, Super Glue)
____Plastic bags (assorted Ziplocs)
____Potty kit (TP, antibacterial wipes)

____Tarp with cord & 4 stakes
____Stove fuel
____First-aid kit
____Maps
____50' 3/8" rope
____Folding saw

Optional items
____Portable/weather radios
____Small carabiner(s)
____Trowel

Notes:
- Your tarp should be around twelve-foot by twelve-foot and have ten feet of cord attached to each corner.
- Fifty feet of rope is used to secure food pack.
- Fifty feet of cord is used to hang tarp and/or clothes line.
- A large camp knife or small axe can be used to split wood.
- Plastic bags work for leftovers or trash.
- Whether to carry any radio, weather or AM/FM is your choice.
- Two-way radios can be used with larger groups.
- A carabiner is handy for hanging food.

Appendix 7

Cook Gear

Checklist
___ 2 pots with lids
___ Large spoon
___ Measuring cup
___ Dish rag/scrubby
___ Antibacterial wipes/lotion

___ Hot pads
___ Cook knife
___ Dish soap
___ Dish towels
___ Vegetable oil

Optional items
___ Skillet
___ Coffee press
___ Pasta spoon
___ Tongs
___ Bake pan
___ Reflector oven

___ Coffee pot
___ Spatula
___ Ladle
___ Foil
___ Cutting board
___ Paper napkins

Notes:
- Pots should be large enough to accommodate the group size.
- Pots should nestle together. Hot pads for handling cookware.
- Measuring cup is for meal preparation. It can also be used as a ladle.
- Dish soap, scrubby, and towel needed to maintain a clean camp. Antibacterial wipes/lotion is nice to keep the cook clean.
- Vegetable oil is used in many recipes.
- The skillet and spatula are used to fry your fish or make pan bread. Which utensils to bring will be dependent on your meal selection.
- If you don't drink coffee, the coffee pot can be used to heat or haul water.
- Foil has many uses but may not be needed. Bake pan is needed only if you plan on baking biscuits or desserts.
- The reflector oven can be used to bake dishes or as a wind break for the stove.

Appendix 8

Personal Gear

Checklist
A pack large enough to hold/carry the following gear:
___Sleeping bag
___Sleeping pad
___Clothing (in a ditty or dry bag)
___Towel
___Rain gear – hooded coat, pants
___Canteen or bottle (Nalgene), Quart/Liter capacity
___Head lamp with fresh batteries
___Small flashlight with fresh batteries
___Personal toilet paper/wipes in Ziploc bag
___Mess kit – cup, plate, bowl, fork, spoon
___Personal hygiene – toothbrush, tooth paste, comb, deodorant, lip balm, meds, other.
___Sunscreen
___Aloe/lidocaine lotion
___Multi-tool or pocket knife
___Matches or fire starter
___Identification/Permit
___Camera
___Seat or pad
___Repellant

Optional items
____Fishing gear – rod, reel, tackle, license, filet knife
____Book
____Compact binoculars
____Glasses case
____Day hike/fanny pack

Note:
- Sleeping bag, clothes, and towel should be in water-tight bag(s).
- Head lamp alone will work, but it's nice to have a backup.
- A flashlight shines further for spotting at night.
- A deep dish will work as a bowl or a plate.
- A "spork" can be used to replace the fork and spoon.
- Hygiene items are a personal preference.
- Aloe lotion with lidocaine is recommended for sunburn or bug bites.
- Fishing gear and a book will be dependent on personal activities.
- Binoculars are great for spotting wildlife or an open campsite.
- Glasses case to protect your glasses

Appendix 9

Meal Suggestions

Breakfast

- Sweet rolls (first morning)
- Instant oatmeal
- Dried fruit
- Cereal or granola with dry milk
- Powdered (instant) breakfast mixed with dry milk
- Dehydrated breakfast packet(s)
- Breakfast bars
- Pop Tarts
- Pancakes and syrup

Lunch

- Packaged soups
- Dehydrated soups, chilis, and stews
- Sausage and cheese
- Thin buns, pita pockets, or tortillas with:
  - Ham Salad - dice a Spam slice and mixed it with a packet of mayonnaise.
  - Chicken salad - mix chicken (Tyson, 7 oz.) with two packets of mayo, serves two.
  - Tuna salad – prepackaged (Sunkist, 2.6 oz.) or tuna (Sunkist, 2.6) with one packet of mayo, serves one or (Sunkist 6.4 oz.) with two packets of mayo, serves two.
  - Ham sandwich, Spam slice with brown mustard.
  - Peanut butter and jelly.

Snacks

The following can be used as "on the go" lunches or as snacks.

- Trail mix
- Dried fruit
- Granola/fruit/energy bars

- Candy bars
- Sunflower seeds
- Beef jerky/sticks
- String cheese

Suppers

By campfire

Meats
- Hamburgers
- Bratwurst
- Boneless chicken breast
- Boneless pork chops
- Boneless steak
- Fresh fish fried in a skillet, breaded and/or seasoned, in a little oil or water

Vegetables
- Baked potatoes
- Corn on the cob

Foil packs
- Any vegetables with water
- Diced potatoes with oil/water and seasoning
- Diced sausage, Spam, chicken or dried beef, with diced potatoes, and any vegetable. Add seasoning and oil/water.
- Fresh fish with seasoning and water

On the camp stove

Rice dishes
- **Jambalaya with sausage** – One 8 oz. box jambalaya mix, 12 to 14 oz. chorizo or Andouille sausage: Add 2½ cups of water to a pot. Add rice mix, cut up meat, and a dash of oil. Heat to boil. Remove from heat and stir, cover and let sit. Reheat and stir every five to ten minutes until done, thirty to forty minutes; serves three to four.
- **Chicken and rice** – One 6 oz. box Uncle Ben's Original rice, 7 oz. Tyson chicken packet or 8 oz. precooked diced chicken: Add 2 cups of water to a pot. Add seasoning packet, rice mix, meat and a dash of oil. Heat to boil. Remove from heat and stir, cover and let sit. Reheat and stir every five to ten minutes until done, thirty to forty minutes; serves two to three.
  Note: The precooked chicken can be made by sautéing diced chicken in butter or by baking chicken breasts and dicing when cooled. Freeze until needed.
- **Sausage and rice** - One cup white, brown, or long-grain rice, 8 oz. summer sausage, two packets brown or home-style gravy: Add 2½ cups water and gravy to a plastic bag, mix. Pour in a pot and add rice mix, cut up sausage, and a dash of oil. Heat to boil. Remove from heat and stir, cover and let sit. Reheat and stir every five to ten minutes until done, thirty to forty minutes; serves two to three.
- Stir Fry - One cup white, brown, or long-grain rice, 8 oz. precooked stir fry of your choice: Add 2½ cups of water and rice in a pot with a dash of oil. Heat to boil. Remove from heat and stir, cover and let sit. Reheat and stir every five to ten minutes until done, thirty to forty minutes. Place precooked stir fry in a separate pot. As the stove becomes available warm up the mixture. Alternate pots until both are done. Serves two to three.
- As a side – ½ cup dry rice of your choosing: Add 1¼ cup water and rice to a pot with a dash of oil. Heat to boil. Remove from heat and stir, cover and let sit. Reheat and stir every five to ten minutes until done, thirty to forty minutes. Serves two.

Pastas
- **Italian sausage in marinara** – 8 oz. precooked mild Italian sausage, 8 oz. spaghetti or linguini noodles, 16 oz. of sauce in soft side package (Poma, Hunts), or 6 oz. tomato paste repackaged to a plastic bag, 1 packet spaghetti sauce mix, 4 oz. parmesan cheese or fresh mozzarella: Mix in 1 packet of sauce mix to tomato sauce or make sauce by adding 1 ½ cups water to tomato paste. Mix thoroughly in plastic bag. Add mixture to a pot and add meat, bring to a boil. Remove from heat and stir, cover and let sit. Reheat and stir every five to ten minutes until warmed through. In another pot bring two quarts of water to a boil. Add noodles and return to boil. Remove from heat and stir, cover and let sit until al dente, drain and serve. Serve meat sauce over noodles topped with cheese. Serves two to three.
- **Chicken marinara** – Same as above but substitute 7 oz. Tyson chicken packet or 8 oz. precooked diced chicken for the meat. Serves two to three.
- **Chicken Alfredo** – Same as above but substitute Alfredo sauce for spaghetti sauce. Alfredo sauce is a little testier and requires simmering to thicken up and it will scorch if you are not stirring constantly. Serves two to three.
- **Beef tips over egg noodles** – 8 oz. precooked beef tips with sliced mushrooms and brown gravy, 8 oz. egg noodles: Bring one to two quarts of water to a boil. Add noodles and return to boil. Remove from heat and stir, cover and let sit until tender, drain and serve. Place precooked beef tips in a separate pot. As the stove becomes available warm up the mixture. Serve the meat sauce over egg noodles. Serves two to three.
Note: To make the beef tips brown the diced beef in butter, mix packet of brown gravy mix in cold water then add to the beef, simmer until beef is tender, add 4 oz. cut up mushrooms and cook until soft. Freeze until needed.
- **Chicken and gravy over egg noodles** – Same as above but substitute 7 oz. Tyson chicken pack or 8 oz. precooked diced chicken and packet of chicken gravy mix for the meat, 8 oz. egg noodles. Serves two to three.

- **Salisbury Sausage** – 6 oz. box Salisbury Hamburger Helper, ¼ cup dry milk, 8 oz. cut up summer sausage, 1 cup mixed vegetables: Follow package directions but substitute sausage for ground beef. Add vegetables toward the end. Serves two to three.
- **Mac and Cheese Supreme** – 7 oz. box of Mac n Cheese, 4 tsp. dry milk, 4 tbsp. butter or 2 tbsp. oil, 6.4 oz. tuna packet, and 1 cup of peas: Make the Mac n Cheese as directed on the box. Substitute dry milk for liquid milk by adding ¼ cup water to plastic bag containing the dry milk, mix. Add oil or butter. Add tuna and peas. Heat until warmed through. Serves two to three.
- **Mac and Cheese Royale** – Same as above but substitute 8 oz. cut up summer sausage and 1 cup corn for the meat and vegetable. Serves two to three.
- **Mac and Cheese American** – Same as above but substitute four cut up hot dogs and 1 cup green beans for the meat and vegetable. Serves two to three.

Mashed potatoes

- **Chicken and gravy over mashed potatoes** - 7 oz. Tyson chicken pack or 8 oz. precooked diced chicken, packet of chicken gravy mix, 2 cups dry instant mashed potato (to make 3 cups prepared), 3 Tbsp. butter or 1½ Tbsp. of oil, 2/3 cup dry milk (to make 1 cup of milk): In a plastic bag add gravy mix to 1 cup of water, mix. Pour mix into a pot and add meat, bring to a boil. Remove from heat and stir, cover and let sit. Reheat and stir every five to ten minutes until thickened and warmed through. In a separate pot bring 2 cups of water and butter or oil to a boil, remove from heat. Add 1 cup water to bag containing dry milk, mix. Add milk mixture and dry potatoes to pot and mix. Serve meat and gravy over mashed potatoes. Add 1 cup of a vegetable to the mix if you wish. Serves two to three.

- **Beef or sausage and gravy over mashed potatoes** - Same as above but substitute 8 oz. precooked beef, 8 oz. cut up sausage or two 4.5 oz. packets of dried beef for the chicken. Substitute brown or home-style gravy for the chicken gravy. Serves two to three.

Tortillas
- **Beef burritos and rice** – 8 oz. precooked burrito meat with seasoning, four 8-inch or 10-inch tortillas, ½ cup dry rice of your choosing, 4 oz. grated cheese, four packets taco sauce from fast food joint: Add 1¼ cup water and rice to a pot with a dash of oil. Heat to boil. Remove from heat and stir, cover and let sit. Reheat and stir every five to ten minutes until done, thirty to forty minutes. Place precooked burrito meat in a separate pot. As the stove becomes available warm up the mixture. Alternate pots until both are done. Wrap meat, cheese, sauce, and rice in a tortilla or the rice can be served on the side. Serves two to three.
- **Beef/Chicken Fajitas and rice** – Same as above but substitute the meat with 8 oz. precooked fajita meat of your choosing and fajita seasoning. Omit the cheese if you wish. Serves two to three.

Soup/stew
There is a variety of soups you can use for wilderness meals. Remember no cans, so you will want to purchase soup-mix packets. The brand you choose is your choice. Knorr and Lipton are good options. These soups can be prepared as directed or you can turn them into a heartier meal/stew by adding ingredients or adding less water. The below recipes are designed for the smaller soup packets that make 3 to 4 cups per packet. *Serves two to three.*
- ***Chicken, chicken noodle*** – Add 7 oz. Tyson chicken pack or 6 oz. precooked diced chicken. Mix in a cup of carrots or corn. They call it "booyah" in Northeastern Wisconsin.
- ***Beef*** – Add 6 oz. precooked beef, cut up sausage, or 4.5 oz. dried beef. Mix in a cup of peas.

- **Pork** – Add two 3 oz. cut up Spam slices, or four cut up hot dogs.
- **Split pea** - Add two 3 oz. cut up Spam slices, or four cut up hot dogs. Mix in a cup of carrots.
- **Potato** – Add two 3 oz. cut up Spam slices, or four cut up hot dogs.
- **Vegetable** – Have fun with this. It doesn't have to be all vegetable. You can add any combination of the above ingredients or you can use up any leftovers.

To prepare the above, add measured amount of water to a pot, add soup mix, meat, and a vegetable, heat to boil. Remove from heat and stir, cover and let sit. Reheat and stir every five to ten minutes until done, twenty to thirty minutes.

- **Instant Mashed Potato Soup** – Follow box directions for 2 cups (four servings) of instant mashed potatoes. Place measured amount of water in a pot, add 1 cup diced Spam/ham/hot dog, 1 cup cooked carrots, 1 tbsp. oil. Heat to a boil, allow meat and carrots to warm through, remove from heat. Add measured amount of instant mashed potatoes and three times the milk the recipe calls for. Mix thoroughly. *Serves two to three.*

You can bake rolls, bannock or corn bread the night before and serve with the soups.

Box Dinners *(assorted)*
Ground beef can be substituted with precooked beef, dried beef or cut up sausage. Precooked diced chicken or Tyson chicken packets can be used in the chicken recipes and Sunkist tuna packets work in the tuna recipes. Follow package directions. *Serves three to four.*

Appetizers

Sausage - Cut up and serve as needed.
Cheese block - Cut up and serve as needed.
Crackers - Keep in protected area of pack. Serve with above.
Cocktail bread – Rye, pumpernickel, or sour dough. Great with any of the below dips or spread.
Pita bread cut up for dipping - Great with any of the below dips.
Humus/guacamole/vegie dip - Keep in protected area of pack.
Cheese spread - Keep in protected area of pack.

Desserts/Baked Goods

Pudding - Chocolate, butterscotch, pistachio, etc. To pack - place the pudding mix packet in a plastic bag large enough to hold all the finished ingredients. Add small plastic bag with measured amount of dry milk to it. To make – remove pudding packet from bag. Place dry milk with measured amount of water in the bag, mix. Add pudding mix to bag and continue mixing (squish it around in the bag). Set aside until ready to serve. You can eat it right out of the bag.

Bannock (pan) bread – To pack; place in a plastic bag large enough to hold all finished ingredients; 1 cup flour, 1 tsp, baking powder, ¼ tsp. salt, (or substitute previous with 1 cup Bisquick), ¼ cup dry milk powder. To mix; add 1 tbsp., oil to bag and start adding water slowly (about ½ cup) while mixing (squish it around in the bag). Add only enough water to make a stiff batter; you do not want runny batter. Add batter to well-oiled bake pan or skillet. Bake as described in Chapter Five. Serve with jelly, maple syrup, or honey or keep for tomorrow's dinner.

Biscuits - To pack; place in a plastic bag large enough to hold all finished ingredients; 2 cups flour, 1 tbsp. baking powder, 1 tsp. salt, (or substitute previous with 2¼ cup Bisquick), ¼ cup dry milk powder. To mix; add 1 tbsp. oil to bag and start adding water slowly (about 2/3 cup) while mixing (squish it around in the bag). Add enough water to make dough that will stand on its own. Add golf ball sized dollops of dough to oiled bake pan. Bake in a hot reflector oven until golden as described in Chapter Five. Makes nine biscuits.

Corn bread - Find a corn bread mix that does not require eggs (Martha White). Package, prepare, and bake as described above. Serve with jelly, maple syrup, or honey. You can also make it as pan bread.

Muffin slab - Find a muffin mix that does not require eggs (Betty Crocker, Martha White). Package, prepare, and bake as described above.

Appendix 10

Fishing Tackle

The following is a condensed listing of possible fishing tackle you may want to bring. The amount of tackle you bring will be dependent on the species of fish you are fishing for, your fishing technique, and the duration of your trip. Remember to bring only the minimum that you will need.

One method is to make a list of the items you think you will need and then divide it in half. With the exception of your filet knife, pliers/forceps, and stringer everything else should fit in a nine-inch by six-inch or similar tackle box. Double-sided boxes are also nice.

<u>*Accessories*</u>
8#-10# fishing line
Filet knife
Needle nose pliers or forceps
Stringer
Nail clipper
Tape measure
Fish gripper
2 - 1-gal. plastic bags

<u>*Terminal tackle*</u>
Snap swivels
Assorted hooks
2-way swivels
3-way swivels
Assorted sizes steel split shot
Walking sinkers
Slip bobbers
Lindy rig
Bottom bouncers
20# steel leaders (pike)
Steel sinkers, 1 & 2 oz. (lake trout)

Lures
Inline spinners
   #3 and #5 Mepps or similar
      Buck Tail, Black Fury, Giant Killers
   Colors - gold, silver, chartreuse
Floating minnow plugs
   #7 and #8 Rapala or similar (walleye, bass)
      Shad Rap, Original, Thunder Sticks,
      Husky Jerk, Lazy ike, Rebel Craw
   #11 and #13 Rapala or similar (pike, lake trout)
      Shad Rap, Original, Husky Jerk
   Colors - silver/white, blue/white, gold/black,
      blue/silver, orange/white, chartreuse, fire tiger
Spoons
   Daredevils, Cleos, Swedish Pimples, Johnson, Sutton,
   Acme Kastmaster, Crocodile (lake trout),
   Deep Tail Dancers (lake trout)
   Colors – silver, red/white, black/white, blue/silver,
      chartreuse/silver
Top water plugs
   Chug Bug, PopR, Jitterbugs Skitterpops
Spinnerbaits
   Beetle Spin
Rattlers
   Rat L Trap

Jigs/soft baits
Assorted color ball jigs
Assorted tube jigs
Assorted colors artificial bait
  3-inch to 5-inch leeches, crawlers, twister tails, tubes,
    flukes, crawdads
  Colors – white, black, chartreuse
Scented soft baits
   Gulp, Yum

Appendix 11

Contacts / Resources

Superior National Forest
Forest Headquarters
8901 Grand Ave. Place
Duluth, MN 55808
218-626-4300

Gunflint Ranger Station
Grand Marais, MN
218-387-1750

Kawishiwi Ranger Station
Ely, MN
218-365-7600

La Croix Ranger Station
Cook, MN
218-666-0020

Tofte Ranger Station
Tofte, MN
218-663-8060

Boundary Waters Canoe Area Wilderness
Information
Superior National Forest
www.recreation.gov
218-626-4300

Reservations
877-444-6777
www.fs.fed.us/superior/special places

Border Crossing
U.S. Customs and Border Protection
www.cbp.gov

Fishing License
Minnesota Department of Natural Resources
www.dnr.state.mn.us

Quetico Provincial Park
Park Headquarters
108 Saturn Ave.
Atikokan, ON, P0T 1C0
807-597-2735

Information
Ontario Parks
800-ONTARIO (800-668-2746)
www.ontarioparks.com

Reservations
888-ONT-PARK (888-668-7275)
www.ontarioparks/reservations.com

Border Crossing and RABC Permit
Canadian Border Services Agency
CANPASS – RABC
www.cbsa.gc.ca/prog/canpass/rabc

Fishing License
Ministry of Ontario Natural Resources
www.mnr.gov.on.ca

Law Enforcement

In an emergency dial 911

Cook County Sheriff
218-387-3030

Lake County Sheriff
218-834-8885

St. Louis County Sheriff
218-749-6010

Ontario Provincial Police
Atikokan
807-597-2255

Maps

National Geographic Maps
P.O. Box 4357
Evergreen, CO 80437-4357
800-962-1643
natgeomaps.com

W. A. Fisher Co.
123 Chestnut
P.O. Box 1107
Virginia, MN 55792
218-741-9544
fishermaps.com

McKenzie Maps
8479 E. Frye Rd
Minong, WI 54859
800-749-2113
mckenziemaps.com

Voyageur Maps
voyageurmaps.com

Acknowledgements

I cannot believe that anyone has ever written a book on their own. From the very first thought of a book, one that was put forth by the corps, numerous ideas and details have been explored. The knowledge and experience that is put forth in this book is not mine alone. My role was to merely put them on paper. I am a student of life and I can learn from others. The collaboration within the corps was vital to this book being completed.

Therefore, I thank the corps, my family and friends who have accompanied me during our numerous trips to the Boundary Waters and on many a wilderness adventure. My wife, Mary; my sons, Dan, Steve, and Pete; my brothers, Mike and Rod; my nieces and nephews, Emily, Jean, Pete, Nick, Tom, Bob, and Chris. And even my great-nephews, Stone and Peter.

We have taken hundreds of pictures during our trips. Just a few were used in this book. Special thanks go out to Nick, Pete, and Tom for their contributions.

All of this would be for naught without the help of the professionals. The editing, formatting, and constructive guidance provided by Mike Dauplaise, Bonnie Groessl, and Julie Rogers of M&B Global Solutions Inc. made it all possible.

My most sincere thanks to all.

Rich Annen
January 2017

About the Author

Rich Annen is the Training and Safety Officer for the De Pere, Wisconsin, Fire Department and has been a professional firefighter for more than thirty-five years. He has enjoyed traveling throughout the United States and Canada with family and friends his entire life.

Rich Annen

Made in the USA
Lexington, KY
16 April 2018